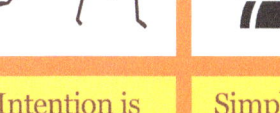		
Intention is the key	Simple things with meanings	Emptying everything	What is sweet and bitter? when?

ALCHEMY
OF MEANINGS AND HAPPINESS

PRACTICAL ETHICAL SPIRITUAL SUFI STORIES TODAY

- CHRISTIANS
- MUSLIMS,
- JEWS
- BUDDHISTS
- HINDUS
- EVERYONE WHO VALUES THE DEEPER MEANINGS

Happy man

Dr. Y. J. Kumek

Animals as teachers	Escorting your belief, the most valuable	Easy to be angry, difficult to be nice!	Art of living together

Cover images © Shutterstock.com

Kendall Hunt
publishing company

www.kendallhunt.com
Send all inquiries to:
4050 Westmark Drive
Dubuque, IA 52004-1840

Copyright © 2018 by Y.J. Kumek

ISBN 978-1-5249-7657-6

All rights reserved. No part of this publication may be reproduced, stored in a retrieval system, or transmitted, in any form or by any means, electronic, mechanical, photocopying, recording, or otherwise, without the prior written permission of the copyright owner.

Published in the United States of America.

PREFACE

This book brings into our current life important Sufi teachings in a one-page story format. Each story has the first paragraph as the story and the second paragraph as the meanings and interpretations from the practice. In this book, the stories aim to use contemporary life encounters with Sufi meanings and interpretations. The stories have been compiled from ethnographic field work in different Sufi communities of New York, Boston, Pittsburgh, Chicago, Toronto, Istanbul, and Cairo.

Y. J. Kumek, PhD
State University of New York (SUNY)
May 27, 2018

CONTENTS

Preface . . . . *iii*

1. Ant and the Sufi 1
2. One Dollar Coffee Machine 2
3. Coffee Machine and Serving 3
4. Cookies and Scripture 4
5. Sufi Argues with His Wife 5
6. The Best Voice 6
7. Looking at the Mirror 7
8. Sufi and Value of the Book 8
9. Evil and the Sufi 9
10. Number of Angels and the Sufi 10
11. The Door and the Responsibility 11
12. Death and the Sufi 12
13. Coffee Machine and Generosity 13
14. Sufi and His Sufi Mother 14
15. Sufi and Garlic 15
16. Sufi and the Elevator 16
17. Sufi and His Father 17
18. Sufi and Serving 18
19. Sufi and Serving Coffee 19
20. Sufi and Her Pocket 20
21. Sufi and Oranges in His Pocket 21
22. Sufi and People's Jealousy 22
23. The Sufi and the Trip 23
24. When and Where to Die and the Sufi 24
25. Sufi and the Bitterness and Sweetness 25
26. Sufi and Hiding 26
27. Heart and the Sufi 27
28. The Sufi and the Sunglasses 28

29. The Sufi on the Beaches of Miami 29
30. Sufi and Eating 30
31. Sufi Who Talks a Lot When He Is at Fault 31
32. Death and the Sufi 32
33. Being Lonely Among the Sufis 33
34. Backbiting and Arguing..34
35. Silence and the Sufi..35
36. The External and the Daytime 36
37. The Internal and the Night 37
38. Required Divorce 38
39. Two Cats and the Sufi...39
40. Cat, Mouse, and the Sufi 40
41. Sufi and the Professor..41
42. Evil and the Pregnancy 42
43. Bad Word and the Sufi...43
44. Bad Smell and Thinking..44
45. Shouting and the Sufi...45
46. Glass Cup and the Sufi Teacher..................................46
47. Sufi and the Ocean 47
48. Man with One Leg and Man with One Eye...........................48
49. Sufi and the Eyeglasses...49
50. The Ant and the Carpet 50
51. Sufi and the Right Answer.......................................51
52. Sufi and Choosing His Prospective Wife..........................52
53. Sufi and Not Flying...53
54. Sufi and Burping..54
55. King and the Sufi...55
56. Sufi, Change, and God 56
57. Sufi and the Preface of a Book..................................57
58. Sufi and the Satan 58
59. Sufi and the Handyman 59
60. The Sufi and the Questions 60
61. The Funny Handyman and the Sufi 61
62. Sufi and the Deaf Man 62
63. Sufi Teacher and the Kids 63
64. Sufi and the Literalist 64
65. Sufi and Different Languages 65
66. Sufi and Her Book...66

CONTENTS

67. Sufi and Phrases on the Tongue 67
68. Sufi and the Huffing and Puffing Handyman 68
69. The Lucky Sufi... 69
70. Sufi and the Magic 70
71. Milk, Pee, and the Sufi 71
72. Rotation of the Days and the Sufi............................. 72
73. Sufi and Her Book... 73
74. Sufi and Two Cases.. 74
75. Third World Countries and the Sufi............................ 75
76. Communication with the Unknowns and Unseen 76
77. The Sufi and the Pancreatic Cancer 77
78. Sufi and Her Teacher 78
79. The Rich Sufi and His Teacher's Food 79
80. The Teacher and Humbleness 80
81. Sufi and the Hindu 81
82. Sufi and the Safety.. 82
83. Sufi and the Escort 83
84. Firefighters, Roof Rats, and the Sufis........................ 84
85. The Rich Sufi, Online Shopping, and the Poor Sufi 85
86. Sufi and Temporary Things..................................... 86
87. Sufi Teacher and the Clock 87
88. Sufi and Perception... 88
89. Now I Understood! and the Sufi................................ 89
90. The Level of Union and the Evil 90
91. The Uber Driver, Cursing, and the Coffee...................... 91
92. The Crying Boy and the Sufi 92
93. The Huffing and Puffing Man and the Sufi 93
94. Sufi, Cat, and the Natural Habitat............................ 94
95. Rain Drops and the Sufi....................................... 95
96. Focused Eating and the Sufi 96
97. The Nice Flower and the Eye................................... 97
98. The Marriage Problem and the Sufi 98
99. The Fried Chicken, the Mother, and the Sufi 99
100. Eating Meat and the Sufi 100
101. Cat and the Garage Door...................................... 101
102. The Sufi and Understanding His Wife.......................... 102
103. "Staying Out of Trouble" and the Sufi 103
104. The Sufi, Child, and Disturbance 104

105. The Sufi and the Floating Wood Log on the Sea. 105
106. The Sufi and the Cat in the Hood of the Car. 106
107. Final Stage of the Fireworks and the Sufi 107
108. The Sufi and the Oppression 108
109. Crying, Child, and the Sufi 109
110. The Sufi, Body, and Mindfulness 110
111. Art of Living and the Sufi 111

Bibliography 113

Glossary 117

Acknowledgments. 127

About the Author 128

Index 129

ALCHEMY OF MEANING AND HAPPNESS

1. Ant and the Sufi

There was an ant who was going for pilgrimage. A Sufi saw him and asked him:

> Sufi: Where are you going?
>
> Ant: To the holy sites.

The Sufi laughs and says:

> Sufi: I don't think you will make it. The holy sites are a thousand miles away from where we are right now.
>
> Ant: I know that, but I have the intention.

The Sufi feels so ashamed about the ant's answer and declares the ant to be his teacher.

In Sufi practice, intentions precede actions. If a person intends always for the good and beneficial, God rewards the person according to the person's intention. If a person prays or gives charity to the poor with the intention of showing off to people or to gain some worldly benefit, the person can get what she or he wants in the world, the tag. After death, the person can be punished due to not acting sincerely. Also, in practice, Sufis commonly observe nature, animals, and plants and try to learn from them to increase their spiritual development.

The ant going to pilgrimage

2. One Dollar Coffee Machine

There was a poor Sufi in a mosque. He bought a small coffee machine for a dollar and he put it in the mosque. While he was staying in the mosque, he was drinking coffee by himself. If other people came to the mosque he used to give the leftover coffee to them. As time passed, people started respecting him because he was so generous and giving coffee to everyone. The Sufi gained a reputation as the "respectable coffee maker of the mosque."

Similarly, our egos are similar to cheap coffee machines. As the ego gets responsibility and recognition by God, it gains value. Power, responsibility, and positions bring recognition. If one wants to be recognized by God, a person should maintain humbleness and appreciation of the Divine.

A simple coffee machine

3. Coffee Machine and Serving

As people were coming to the mosque, everyone was asking for coffee from the famous Sufi coffee maker. The Sufi was getting upset. He was being disturbed while he was praying as people were coming and asking coffee from him. One day, he decided to put the coffee machine outside at the serving table. If people want it, they can make their own coffee and they won't disturb the Sufi. People started making their own coffees without disturbing the Sufi. The Sufi said to himself, "I don't care if someone steals the coffee machine, I can buy another one. It is cheap."

Likewise, our egos are cheap coffee machines. If we don't hoard it for ourselves but give it away to serve others to please God, a cheap self can have a high value. If we try to hold our egos tightly the disturbances will increase. Therefore, one should let it go in order to taste the pleasure and satisfaction of serving others.

4. Cookies and Scripture

One day a Sufi was reading and memorizing the scripture, the Quran. He spent a good amount of time with the sacred Book. Then, he took a break for coffee. As soon as he went next to the coffee machine, he saw his favorite cookie next to the coffee machine. He said to himself, "There is no one in the mosque except me. Who brought this cookie? I know this cookie is not local. You need to order it online." He indulged in deep thinking . . .

Sometimes, in the practice, miracles can be called cookies. Cookies may come in different forms as someone engages oneself with practice, reading the Quran, memorizing it, praying, or fasting . . .

The question is: Is the cookie healthy? Meaning that, is it an encouragement by God on the path? Or, is it a test or trial from God to see if the person on the path will be arrogant by claiming supernatural incidents and try to be superior to their fellow human beings.

5. Sufi Argues with His Wife

One day, a Sufi was in an argument with his wife. During the fight he decided to discuss some of their marriage problems.

> Sufi: I need to meet with you to talk.
>
> His wife: You are probably going to tell me how bad I am!
>
> Sufi: Probably, you already told to your friends and my kids how bad I am, so you took the precedence. Congratulations!
>
> His Wife: You claim to be a Sufi and you think about your reputation. Shame on you!
>
> Sufi: You think you are pious. Please stop pretending to be pious and naïve.

Sufi was now thinking. He said to himself, "I am now heading toward a dead end. I am already receiving a lot of texts from her on my phone. If I don't say anything then she will think that she won and I will hear about it for the rest of my life." He was thinking, "What should I do?" Then, he said to his wife:

> Sufi: I wanted to meet with you to tell you how much I appreciate you and I love you. That was the reason . . .

The argument was over. Sufi said, "Alhamdulillah (thanks to God), that was a good thought that Allah gave it to me. I was heading toward a dead end."

In Sufi marital relationships, the spouse is always right. The husband's position is to always be silent and passive in any disputes, forgive, don't make a big deal, and move on.

6. The Best Voice

There was a man in the mosque and he thought he had the best voice when he used to sing to call people to prayer.[1] As soon as he would sing the prayer call, the people in the mosque would leave the mosque in order to not hear his voice until he was done. They waited outside and then came back. He actually had a very bad voice. One day, this man came to the Sufi in the mosque and brought the recording of a famous prayer singer and said, "Can you please listen to this famous singer in the Kabah and tell me who sings the prayer call better? Me or him?"

Sometimes, the spiritual diseases can become the character of a person if there is no fellow friend telling the person of his or her mistakes. Therefore, it is a practice to have friends, not wives or husbands, to tell you your mistakes rather than simply praising your achievements. One Sufi says, "I love a friend who warns me about a scorpion on my chest. Why should I get angry with her?"

---

1. Adhan.

7. Looking at the Mirror

There was a messy Sufi who did not like to look at the mirror. He used to think, "When I see myself in the mirror, it really makes me uncomfortable—the messy hair, untrimmed moustache, uncombed beard, and un-ironed shirts." He used to avoid looking at himself in the mirror.

Similarly, our internal messiness is ugly in its essence. Allah created everyone physically beautiful. Arrogance, hatred, anger, and jealousy are the essence of ugliness. If the person does not have mirrors to reflect on those, then that is the real problem.

8. Sufi and Value of the Book

There was a poor Sufi in a mosque to whom people used to give money for his survival. One day, a man was reading an historical rare prayer litany book. This Sufi saw this book and approached this man.

    Sufi: Can I buy this book from you?

The man smiled sarcastically to the Sufi and said: "I know that you don't have money. How can you pay for this book?"

The Sufi showed a miracle and put his hand in his pocket and took out fresh bills worth a thousand dollars all bunched together and gave them to the man.

The man was shocked and said: "Here is the book. It is a gift from me. I don't want the money."

In this story, one can understand that the market value of the book was a few dollars but the Sufi was willing to give thousands of dollars to get the book. The book was about prayers and the divine expressions of different prophets such as Abraham, Moses, Jesus, Muhammad, and other saints of God. In Sufism, anything valuable in the relationship with God has a very high price. Sufis don't value anything related to this world but rather the Divine.

9. Evil and the Sufi

One day, a person saw a Sufi in the mosque praying. He approached him and said:

> The man: I want to talk to you about something important.

This man was so disturbed by the problems in the world—its injustices and evil.

> He continued and said: I am so disturbed by what is happening in the world!

> The Sufi smiled and said: Is this the reason that you wanted to talk to me?

> The man said: Yes.

> The Sufi said: Did you first ask the same question to Allah for an answer?

The man did not respond but did not seem happy with the Sufi's answer either. Understanding this, the Sufi continued:

> Look! I understand you want to do something. Right?

> The man said: Yes.

> The Sufi: How do you do it? You have ideas, then you put them into action, right?

> The man: Yes.

> The Sufi: So, ask Allah to inspire you with the right and fruitful, and good ideas about what you want to do.

The man seemed a little bit more convinced with the Sufi's logic.

In Sufism, doing good with the inspiration of easiness from Allah is very important. One can ask God to make it easy for the right choice in decision-making. In practice, there is a constant dialogue that is expected between the Divine and humans.

10. Number of Angels and the Sufi

There was a Sufi in the mosque. A man knew him and said to himself, "Let me ask him a question and tease him."

The man: How many angels are in the mosque now?

The Sufi: There are currently 84 angels.

Some of the Sufis can alternate their positions with the unseen and seen world. These alternations can be due to the high quality and quantity of their engagements with the prayers, chanting, and reading scriptures. Although normal people can think that they are weird, these Sufis may not recognize their own abnormality when interacting with others.

11. The Door and the Responsibility

Everyone was coming to listen to the Friday sermon in the mosque. The Sufi was in the mosque as well. He was sitting next to the outside door. The famous assistant priest of the mosque was sitting next to the Sufi. As people were coming inside they were closing the door and locking it by mistake. Each time, the priest was getting up and unlocking the door and telling the people to leave the door open. Another man came in and did the same as the others, closing the door which would then lock itself. Another, another, another . . . The poor priest was getting annoyed and getting up and sitting down . . . The Sufi was watching and smiling . . .

Similarly, there are people who work in the churches, mosques, or temples. They may be externally close to worshipping God but they are actually very distracted and very far away from God. Sometimes the closeness can make the person blind. It can have an opposite effect. A person looking to the brightness of the sun can become blind. Satan was very close to God but lost. Similarly, some Sufis believe that God is so obvious that if people cannot see God then it is because of the blindness due to the clear brightness.

12. Death and the Sufi

There was an announcement in the mosque: "One of the famous members of the mosque died." Everyone was upset and disturbed. The Sufi was smiling. He said to himself, "What a lucky guy! He is going to meet with God. I don't know why these people seem to be so upset."

In the practice, death is not a pain or evil but the joyful moment of meeting with God. As long as the person is always eager to meet with God and pleased and appreciated God all his life, then God also wants to meet with this person. In one of the famous sayings of the Prophet Muhammad, God will treat the person in the way that she will expect to be treated in the afterlife.

13. Coffee Machine and Generosity

There was a poor Sufi in a mosque. He bought a small coffee machine for a dollar and he put it in the mosque. While he was staying in the mosque, he was drinking coffee by himself. If people came to the mosque he used to give the leftover coffee to them. As time passed, people started respecting him because he was giving coffee to everyone. One day, a person brought some cookies and put them next to the coffee on the serving table. The following day, a person brought crackers. Every day now there were some drinks and food in the mosque.

The best way of teaching in practice is being an example rather than preaching to people. The starter of a good action receives from God each individual's rewards as well.

14. Sufi and His Sufi Mother

The Sufi was talking on the phone with his mother who was in another country:

> Sufi Mother: How is the weather over there? Is it winter or summer?
>
> Sufi: It is summer for the person who always follows the path of God. It is always winter for the person who is not on the path.
>
> Sufi Mother: What do you mean? I don't understand.
>
> Sufi: Did you eat garlic or onion?
>
> Sufi Mother: How do you know? I ate onion.

In the practice, garlic, onion, or any bad smell or bad words or actions will repel angels and make spiritual understandings and inspirations difficult. Therefore, in the story above, the Sufi deduced his mom's inability to grasp the spiritual understandings to her engagement with something unpleasant. He was inspired by God to guess about it and he was correct.

15. Sufi and Garlic

There was a Sufi who used to like garlic sausage a lot. One day, he had an important meeting regarding a job interview. Before the meeting, to make him happy, his wife prepared for him the food that he liked the most: garlic sausage. He ate and he was so happy and ready for the meeting. He went and did the interview. He was answering all the questions successfully but he did not feel right and the interview was over. He didn't get the job. He said to himself: "Garlic sausage. I am not going to eat it anymore."

In practice, the angelic beings do not accompany the person if there is a bad smell due to food or anything. The Sufis try to minimize their time in the bathroom due to these reasons. In the above story, the Sufi understood that although everything seemed to be normal, his inability to control himself when it came to the smelly food made him lose the angelic blessings.

16. Sufi and the Elevator

One day, there was a Sufi with a bunch of people in an apartment elevator. The elevator stopped in-between the floors. Everyone was screaming, pushing the elevator buttons frantically. Some of the ladies were crying. The elevator was still not moving.

Sufi was smiling, waiting for people to calm down a little bit.

Finally, Sufi said "I am sorry; can I push the button?"

He then said: "Bismillah—In the name of God."

The elevator started moving.

In practice, everything works and moves with the name of God. The purpose of all prayers in practice and in one's life is to remember this simple but important fact.

17. Sufi and His Father

Sufi was a student in Boston. His family was living in New York. His father loved the Sufi so much that each time the father talked to the Sufi, he used to compose a song and sing it for his son on the phone. His brother and his mother were jealous about this and said: "Look, he doesn't compose any songs for us but only for his son."

The Sufi heard this and said to his mom and brother, "Names are not important but the characters . . ."

It is common to write letters and compose poems and songs for the loved ones in practice, especially for teachers, friends, and family members. It is the expression of appreciation in words. In the above story, the Sufi was saying that it is not important to whom the song was composed but the content of it.

Sufi's father composing poems for his son

18. Sufi and Serving

As people were coming to the mosque, everyone was asking for coffee from the famous Sufi coffee maker. The Sufi was getting upset. He was being disturbed while he was praying as people were coming and asking him for coffee. One day, he decided to put the coffee machine outside at the serving table. If people want it, they can make their own coffee and they won't disturb the Sufi. Although the coffee machine is out on the serving table, people did not make their own coffee. Everything was next to the machine—the raw coffee, the filter, and water. If people came and asked for coffee from the Sufi, he showed them where the coffee machine was and they could make their own coffee. But, people still did not make it.

Similarly, people take pleasure when they are served. In Eastern cultures this concept of serving is very prominent in social and familial relationship. Although being served can lead a person to laziness and dependency, serving someone—giving or making something and putting together a dish to bring—is a common practice to increase brotherhood and sisterhood. There is a famous aphorism in practice that people are slaves of servitude.

19. Sufi and Serving Coffee

One day, Sufi made a coffee. He was smelling the nice, fresh coffee in the morning and taking pleasure from it. He took the pot and started pouring it into a small coffee cup. A few hot drops spilled, he burned himself, and all the pleasure was lost.

Similarly, in the spiritual pleasure, a small—even tiny—drop of arrogance burns all the efforts on the journey. The Prophet says, "A person who has an atom's size of arrogance in one's heart will not enter paradise and smell the fragrance of it." The antidote to arrogance in the journey is humbleness and humility. One can enact this by constantly prostrating and bowing before God and glorifying God. Also, any thoughts or feelings of arrogance should immediately be addressed. If not, it can mutate into an unhealthy cell like a cancer.

The Sufi and serving coffee

20. Sufi and Her Pocket

There was a Sufi. As she put her hand in her jacket pocket, there were candy wrappers, candies, prayer notes, beads, a napkin, some coins, and other things. As she wanted to pray, she didn't want to be disturbed by knowing of the existence of all those things in her pocket. So, she took off this jacket and prayed wearing one with empty pockets.

Similarly, the practice of detachment from the world during the prayers and chanting is very important. One cannot fully achieve the practice of spiritual emptying or discharging if mindful detachment is not present. According to some of the scholars, putting one's hands back in-between each movement during the prayers is the mental reminder of disgust and detachment from all worldly engagements.

Emptying the pockets

21. Sufi and Oranges in His Pocket

There was a Sufi in Alaska. He used to pray in the mosque and loved to give oranges to the kids after each prayer. He used to put his hand in his jacket and hand out a few oranges to the kids. Kids loved him because in the middle of winter they did not know where the Sufi was getting the oranges. One day, kids and the Sufi were again in the mosque. The Sufi needed to go the restroom. He took out his jacket and put it on the hanger. While waiting, the kids were curious and wanted to check his pocket for the oranges. They put their hands into the pocket opening. There were no pockets—just a big hole where the pockets should be.

It is an everyday incident to encounter different supernatural occurrences or miracles in a Sufi's life. Actually, for a Sufi nothing is abnormal on the path of the Infinite. They consider abnormal as people's lack of appreciation of the Divine.

22. Sufi and People's Jealousy

As the Sufi was spending most of his time in the mosque, everyone was getting annoyed with him. People were gossiping and saying, "We are working and this guy is spending all his time here, worshipping." His wife was getting annoyed with him as well because he was spending all his time with worship and she was complaining to him that she always wanted to worship like him but she was not able to do it. The Sufi realized this and said to himself, "What should I do before these people destroy me with their jealousy? I need to hide myself . . . "

It is a very common historical occurrence that jealousy of people always puts the Sufis in jeopardy. Therefore, some try to pretend to be insane. Some leave people altogether and live in the mountains or in caves. Some try to pretend or take the title of being the cleaner of a mosque or a temple.

23. The Sufi and the Trip

Sufi's brother in-law came from California to Cleveland. The Sufi was living in New York.

> He said to his wife: Why don't we visit your brother?
>
> His wife: What a nice husband! Let's go!
>
> Sufi: Do you want your sister to come too?
>
> His wife: That is a great idea!
>
> Sufi: How about your mom? Why don't you take her too?
>
> His wife: Thank you, honey! You are so thoughtful.

A day later...

> Sufi: Honey, I want to come on the trip with you but I don't want to disturb you. You can go as a family with your brother and mom, and chat about your old memories.
>
> His wife: Are you sure? You don't want to come with us?
>
> Sufi: Maybe not this time.
>
> His wife: Okay.

Sufis always prefer spending time with God. Sufi are very jealous about their relationship with God. Any engagement should be really something worthy to disturb these sweet moments of spending time with God in worship. In the above story, the Sufi taught that it was not necessary for him to go because his wife already had company.

24. When and Where to Die and the Sufi

The Sufi's wife in the above story always complained about his indecisiveness when it came to planning trips or vacations. When his wife suggested to the Sufi that they visit her brother, she already had backup plans. The Sufi used to change his mind a lot about going on a trip.

Sufis often contemplate where and when they will die. Before engaging themselves with a trip or to any commitment, they may ask the following questions to themselves for self-reflection: Do I need to go on this trip? Will it benefit my relationship with God? If I die on this trip, what is my intention and how will I answer God? According to the normative beliefs, a person will meet with God in the way and the place where one dies.

25. Sufi and the Bitterness and Sweetness

There was a Sufi who used to eat sweet in the daytime and salty at night. When a person asked the reason he said, "The daytime is already bitter. I need to neutralize it with some sweetness. The nighttime is already sweet and I need to neutralize it with some bitterness."

In practice, there is always longing for the Divine. Due to daily distractions, a person may not find avenues to concentrate on the worship and remembrance of God during the daytime. Therefore, it can be bitter for the ones who are disconnected with God. On the contrary, the nights are releases from worldly duties so there is more time to engage in prayer and remembrance of God. Therefore, it is sweet as long as one uses it to charge and discharge oneself in the spiritual path of God. In practice, worshipping at night has a high value for God.

Balance the sweet night with bitterness and the bitter day with sweetness

26. Sufi and Hiding

One day a Sufi was hiding from the people in the mosque. In his hiding space, he was enjoying the prayer, reflection, and the divine experiences. A lady was in the mosque as well. When the lady saw this Sufi in his hiding spot, she started screaming and ran away. She thought that he was an abnormal being.

In practice, privacy within the public space is a key to maintaining constant companionship with God. If the person does not uphold this notion, he will suffer due to detachment from God. This is a big torture for the ones in practice. Therefore, there is a famous prayer from the Prophet Muhammad: "Oh God! Do not leave me alone even less time than a blinking of an eye."

27. Heart and the Sufi

One day a Sufi was not feeling well. He was trying to focus on his heart. As he looked within the details of his heart, he realized that he was longing for God. Then, he started reading the scripture and prayer and started crying. As he was crying, he started feeling better and said to himself, "Alhamdulillah, thanks be to God." Then, as he was engaged in crying, he felt dehydrated and wanted to drink coffee. He said, "Bismillah, in the name of God," and took a sip. While attempting the second sip, he spilled the coffee on himself and said, "Astagfirullah, forgive me God."

In the teachings of Sufi practice, the heart oscillates in the state of spiritual contraction and expansion, as the names of God are the Contractor and the Expander. When the person feels in contraction in the state of heart, this is a signal or a call for the person to engage in praying and glorification of God through prayer, chanting, or reading the scripture. As the person transforms oneself to the expansion state of the heart, there is always an increased possibility of spiritual arrogance. Therefore, the traveler should constantly be in the state of alertness and humbleness with the notion of "Astagfirullah." In the above story, spilling coffee on oneself can indicate the representation of possible arrogance in mystical understandings.

28. The Sufi and the Sunglasses

There were two Sufis in the mosque. One was rich but used to buy cheap clothes. The other was poor but always wanted to buy expensive clothes. One day, the rich Sufi went to a dollar store to buy sunglasses. Then, he went to the mosque with his new sunglasses. The poor Sufi saw him with his new sunglasses and said: "You look very nice with your expensive Ray-ban[2] sunglasses." The rich Sufi smiled and took the sunglasses and gave them to the poor Sufi as a gift. The poor Sufi was so happy.

Sometimes, on the spiritual path, a person can assume and put a value on something that is invaluable for God. The external can be deceptive when one assesses its real value. The people's attachment to the world, wealth, and luxury are examples of these incorrect assessments.

---

2. An expensive sunglasses brand.

29. The Sufi on the Beaches of Miami

There were two Sufi friends. One was a regular mosque attendee, spending most of his time in the temple, and enjoying the prayers and reading the scriptures. The other was spending most of his time on the beaches of Miami, enjoying the sun, and while enjoying, performing his prayers and readings from the scripture. One day, the regular Sufi wanted to visit the other Sufi. He was worried about his friend's spirituality because he was spending most of his time on the beach. The regular Sufi took a plane and went to Miami and found his friend on the beach. The regular Sufi was very uncomfortable because the beach was not like the mosque. He was walking and looking down and trying to find his friend and not be affected by the naked scenes of the opposite gender. Finally, he found his friend and immediately asked the question: "I really don't understand. How can you pray and read your scripture here?" His friend said: "They are not attractive. I don't look at them."

In normative teachings, an unwanted look, bite, or hearing can affect the heart of the person. There may be some exceptions to the general rule depending on the special circumstance of the person, similar to the story mentioned above.

30. Sufi and Eating

There were two Sufis—Mary and Kimberly. Kimberly saw Mary eating very slowly.

>Kimberly: What are you doing?

>Mary: Eating.

>Kimberly: Why are you eating so slowly?

>Mary: I am thinking and chanting before I take each bite.

Eating is not a separate engagement but, while doing something, a Sufi can fulfill this need of eating. That is the best way. If one sets a separate time for eating, he or she may not get pleasure from it. It is okay to cook good food and it can take time. During the preparation, one can reflect on different types of food given by God. According to practice, eating can take time if the person is thinking on each bite and chanting on it, but at the end he or she can get more pleasure from it.

31. Sufi Who Talks a Lot When He Is at Fault

One day a Sufi was late to the class. The teacher was angry but did not show his anger. Sufi immediately engaged with the class discussion to pretend that he had been there since the beginning of the class. The other students understood this and were annoyed.

Sometimes, the faults can paint the mind and the heart as a result of not accepting one's mistakes. A person on the path is expected to face all mistakes during the course of the day. It should be the accountability of all actions, words, sentences, sounds, sights, and tastes. At the end of the day, the person can self-evaluate all of his or her dealings and whether they were necessary or not. Then, the next day, the person can become more careful. At least he or she can eliminate some of them in the beginning of this new day. For some scholars, one's realization of his or her mistakes is also a positive achievement on the spiritual path. One of the worst levels of the spiritual path is not realizing one's mistakes or not being aware of them.

32. Death and the Sufi

One day the father of a person died and he came to the mosque. He saw the Sufi sitting and reading the scripture. The man said: "I can't sleep. I still think about my father. I don't have any one. I am all alone by myself."

The grief of the loss is very painful. It is normal to be sad and have tears. In Sufi practice, it should be temporary. The grief for the loss should not take over and become dysfunction in the person's life.

Sufis don't see someone's death as loss but gain as one is finally meeting with the Beloved.

33. Being Lonely Among the Sufis

There were a few Sufis together in a temple. They were engaged in remembrance of God, chanting, and prayers. When there was a coffee break two Sufis were talking.

> John: How do you feel? I feel so content and peaceful after the chanting and it was a nice lecture. I got positive energy.

> Justin: I feel so lonely.

One of the spiritual states in the practice is the state of escape or loneliness. The person in this state can desperately burn for being with God. Although the person may be a saint, this person may not be satisfied with the images, rather desiring the Essence. This stage also can be called union with God if it is not transitory, but remains a permanent spiritual state.

34. Backbiting and Arguing

The Sufi was sitting in the mosque. Some people were talking and laughing about the ugliness of a girl. Sufi heard this and was disgusted about their enjoyment of their backbiting, eating the flesh of their sister.[3] When the Sufi heard this conversation, he stepped away from them in order to not listen to them. Next morning, the Sufi entered the mosque. He saw the same people who were laughing, but now were arguing with each other and they were so angry with each other.

In practice, the effect of something evil can manifest itself as another disturbance. The people talked badly about a poor girl and enjoyed it and now they are fighting with each other over some nonsense.

---

3. In practice, it is known that a person who backbites or gossips behind a person and takes pleasure from it for no purpose is behaving in a way similar to eating the dead flesh of that person.

35. Silence and the Sufi

One day a woman attended a Sufi retreat for self-discipline. She saw a friend of hers that she had not seen for a long time. Her friend asked how the Sufi was doing all these years. The Sufi started explaining in detail what had transpired in all those past years.

Finally, it was the Sufi's turn to ask the same question of her friend and said: "So, how have you been? What did you do all these years that I didn't see you?" Her friend replied: "I am sorry. I cannot talk because the teacher in the self-discipline retreat said that you can eat but you can't talk." The Sufi was so annoyed.

There are three main principles on the spiritual path—minimizing talking, eating, and sleeping. In the above story, the teacher in the retreat let the new practitioners eat whatever they wanted but tried to discipline talking only as a method of teaching. In practice it is understood that the amount of talking, eating, and sleeping are all related. In this case of self-discipline training, the teacher focused only on habitual talking. The Sufi was annoyed because her friend let her talk without telling her of the teacher's recommendation at the beginning of their conversation. If the Sufi knew this, she wouldn't have engaged in talking and wouldn't have told her friend in detail about her life.

36. The External and the Daytime

There was a Sufi in the mosque. It was daytime. The weather was gloomy, rainy, and dark. He heard people screaming, fighting, and arguing in the subway station next to the mosque. The Sufi said to himself, "It is either Satan or the self or both."

In Sufi teachings, one of the names of God is the External. God changes the weather, light, sun, night, rain, snow, hot, and cold. In each change, the spiritual state of the person can be affected. If the person is not on the path, all these changes can depress the person. God gives these changes so that the person feels the need to establish a positive meaningful relationship with God, the External. One of the ideal states of a spiritual traveler is that the external changes do not affect one's spiritual state negatively but help to increase the relationship with the One, the External. It is believed that the negative spiritual states of a person are caused either by Satan or the self of the person, or both. Satan or the untrained self or ego gives temptations to do evil. Then the person can execute it if he or she has a weak connection with the Divine.

37. The Internal and the Night

There was a Sufi. After the sunset, she used to gain her power of inspirations and crying. She used to feel different in her spiritual states compared to daytime. She used to allocate her time especially to writing poems, crying, and reading from the scripture at night times.

In Sufi practice, nights are important avenues to establish a very private and secret relationship with the Divine. One can refer to this name of God as the Internal. God knows all the detailed feelings, emotions, and experiences of a person even though sometimes the person cannot differentiate and name them. According to one of the Prophetic traditions, God especially establishes a very intimate and powerful relationship with the person in the last one-third of the night. The person can get benefit of this relationship if the person is awake—not sleeping—and engaged in prayers, chanting, meditation, and reading the scriptures.

38. Required Divorce

One day a Sufi was giving a lecture about divorce. He explained different cases and their outcomes and finally he said, "The only required divorce is between Satan and the self or ego."

In some of the Sufi understandings, the person's self, ego, or mind is a partner of Satan. Satan sends signals to the self and the self takes it[4] and likes to execute it. Some can say that the self and Satan are married because both work toward the path of destruction of the person. When a person starts a spiritual journey the person can aim to divorce Satan and be independent in order to end the abuse. After this divorce, Satan can get angry and can try to hurt this person but the person has the protection order from God through chanting, prayers, and blessings.

---

4. In some traditions, this relationship is depicted by the dwelling or receiver of the spiritual faculties of the person when Satan sends signals, lummahshaytaniyah.

39. Two Cats and the Sufi

There was a Sufi who had two cats and two children. Cats were brother and sister. This Sufi's children were a boy and a girl. The Sufi used to interact with the cats. The female cat was very polite and sensitive. On the other hand, the male cat was very harsh and aggressive. Therefore, the Sufi used to be very polite to the female cat and at the same time he was trying to teach some good manners with discipline to the male cat. The Sufi was thinking about this difference and realized that maybe he should raise his children similarly.

Sufis generally observe different animal behaviors, the gender differences, the ego, the eating habits, and their reactions. They try to take some lesson from different animals in order to implement in their own self's spiritual discipline.

Animals as teachers

40. Cat, Mouse, and the Sufi

A Sufi had a cat in her house. Her cat's name was Sabir. She put that name to him because of his patience. One day, Sabir found a mouse at home and started chasing it. The mouse went into a hole. Sabir went outside the hole and waited there patiently until the next day when the mouse came out. Sufi was watching this and was amazed with her cat's patience and so named her cat Sabir, the patient one. She acknowledged Sabir as one of her teachers in learning patience.

In Sufi practice, it is very important to observe everything—the animals, the objects, the plants, and the changes. Active and critical thinking is an expected methodology to increase one's knowledge on the spiritual path. The knowledge is useless unless the person benefits himself or herself.

41. Sufi and the Professor

One day a Sufi was giving a lecture on the concept of understanding submission, reliance,[5] and surrender in relationship with God. There was a professor who was sitting as a student in the class. The professor did not get what the Sufi was trying to say. A few years later, the Sufi received a phone call from the professor. The professor was crying and said, "I understand what you meant by surrender now. My wife had cancer. I was distraught. She was getting worse in front of me every day in the hospital. I couldn't help her. I thought that I was powerful and confident. She died. I submit and surrender." Sufi was sad.

In practice, it is very important to embody the notion that all of a person's physical and spiritual power is from God. In other words, the person should believe and embody that one cannot even lift his or her arm or be in a good spiritual engagement unless there is a blessing and opening from God. There are phrases that people chant daily to instill this notion for the spiritual traveler. In the above story, the professor trusted and relied on his own power in his dealings with life and he suffered.

---

5. Tawakkul is translated as reliance.

42. Evil and the Pregnancy

There was a girl who used to go to church regularly. She got pregnant. It was very difficult to handle her labor pains. Finally, she delivered her baby. Now, she stopped going to church. She said to herself, "I have been going to church all my life. God did not help me when I was in pain during my labor. I am not going to go to church again."

People have a difficult time when interpreting the evil, pain, and difficulties in life. One of the purposes of the spiritual path is to train the self and ego before encountering the tests of evil, or difficulties in life. If the person does not wear proper clothes in freezing weather the person can lose his organs and limbs. Similarly, there can be people going to church, mosque, synagogue, or temple. If the people do not acquire and embody the self-training of spiritual heart and mind through practicing different rituals, the person can alienate oneself from practice due to not going beyond with the meaning of symbols.

43. Bad Word and the Sufi

There were two kids who were memorizing the Quran. They were playing in the mosque and the Sufi was busy with his reflection. One of the kids said a bad word to another one. The Sufi called the boys and said, "Make a choice. Good word and bad word does not stay at the same time in the heart." A good word and a bad word cannot occupy the same place in one's heart at the same time. If you say a bad word, all the good words and your memorization will leave you.

In practice, a person's intake of good food, good words, or good smells makes a good spiritual heart. One of the best good words is the word of God. The Quran is pure and clean. Therefore, a person cannot touch the Quran before washing oneself. A person will not be able to memorize something purely if his or her tongue and mind are engaged with anger, backbiting, jealousy, and anything that does not concern the person. This notion is much embedded in the advice of the Prophet for the ones who want to memorize the Quran.[6]

---

6. Tirmizi, M. 2007. *Jami At-Tirmizi*. Dar us-Salam.

44. Bad Smell and Thinking

There was an insane person who used to pee on his clothes. With his smelly clothes, he used to come to mosque. People did not want to embarrass him. The places that he passed in the mosque used to smell bad. One day, this person came to the mosque and then left. The Sufi was praying and thinking "Alhamdulillah, he came but it does not smell bad." As soon as he had these thoughts, it started smelling. The Sufi smiled and said to himself, "My bad thoughts . . . "

Sometimes if a person thinks badly about others, or has feelings of arrogance, the bad thoughts may transform into other forms such as bad smells. In the above story, the Sufi's bad thoughts about the person transformed into a bad smell. One day, there was a man who was backbiting about others. He threw up and some chunks of meat came up in his vomit. He went to the Prophet and said that he did not eat meat but he threw up and meat came out. The Prophet said, "That is the flesh of your brother that you backbit".[7]

---

7. Hanbal, Ahmad B. 2012. *Musnad Imam Ahmad Ibn Hanbal.* Dar-Us-Salam Publications.

45. Shouting and the Sufi

There were two people arguing and shouting in the mosque. A Sufi was in the mosque, too. As soon as the Sufi heard their shouting, he left the mosque.

In practice, when there is shouting among people, then that environment is contaminated with bad spirits instead of the angelic beings. Actually, there are verses in the Quran [31:19] that discourage shouting as a way of communication. Bad spirits encourage bad words, shouting, anger, and physical harm. Angelic beings, the Quran, the chanting, and prayer inspire good words and peaceful feelings and tranquility.

46. Glass Cup and the Sufi Teacher

There was a Sufi who had a glass cup. He wanted to throw it in the garbage. When the Sufi teacher understood this he called the student and said: "My son, do not throw the glass to break it but gently put it down. If you get used to breaking things you will not be careful in breaking people's hearts."

In practice, being genuine to people is very important. God is always with the ones whose hearts are broken according to teachings in practice.

47. Sufi and the Ocean

One day, the Sufi was next to the ocean watching the professional divers. There were a few divers diving to very deep parts of the ocean and bringing out some pearls. The divers were connected with a rope to the ship. One day, one of the divers did not want to dive with the rope. He dived. Hours and then days passed but he did not come back. Then, they found out that he was dead. The Sufi was not surprised but sad.

In the above story, the person maybe had a good intention but did not follow the rules and died. Similarly, in Sufi practice, the rope represents the pillars of the faith and practice. The goal is that the person expands on the pillars without destroying or removing the pillars. One of the main pillars is that God is One and Unique. God revealed the Quran. God states about the Divine Self that God is One and Unique in the scriptures. Some can rationalize this belief and some can submit and surrender to it. Sometimes, there can be renderings due to the problems of analogies and language. Therefore, Sufis don't think about the essence of God but they ponder on the attributes of God. Thinking about essence of God removes the rope in the journeys of spiritual excursions.

Diving with the ropes

48. Man with One Leg and Man with One Eye

One day the Sufi was talking with her nephew on the phone. Her nephew lost most of his sight in one of his eyes. This was due to a tumor behind his eyes. Her nephew was upset. He used to be a good-looking man. While talking with her nephew, the Sufi saw a man with one leg using crutches and going to the mosque to pray. She said to her nephew:

> Sufi: Do you prefer to have two eyes—one perfect and the other not seeing well—or do you prefer to have two perfect eyes but only one leg?

> Nephew: It is tough. I prefer what I have now because I don't know if what you describe is more complicated or painful for me.

In practice, appreciation without any complaints in relationship with God is the key. The phrase Alhamdulillah (thank you God) represents this notion of appreciation in the relationship with the Divine in all circumstances. In the above story, the one-legged man was struggling to go to the mosque to pray to God in order to appreciate what he has. Sometimes, people look at what they don't have and complain instead of appreciating what they have and being thankful in their relationship with God.

49. Sufi and the Eyeglasses

One day a Sufi had a dream. In his dream, he saw that his cat jumped on him and grabbed his eyeglasses. The cat was holding the eyeglasses with his teeth. The Sufi grabbed his eyeglasses and pulled them. The cat was holding them tightly and pulling them to the other direction. The Sufi woke up and he said to himself: "What does this mean?" He was thinking and did not understand the meaning. A few days later, he finally made the interpretation as follows.

As the Sufi was on the spiritual journey he was trying to understand everything in life and beyond. But still, he was using some tools to see, understand, and experience. God was inspiring him through experience and angels to remove all of the tools for the pure objective truth. The cat in this case was representing an angelic being attempting to remove the eyeglasses from the Sufi. But the Sufi was still attached to the world and not focused on the manners of the spiritual path. He still wanted to use the tools or the reasons.

Sometimes, the evil-looking incidents have a purpose in life. Sometimes they are coming with a good purpose similar to Rumi's violent guest poem. The person sometimes struggles and aspires to do something bad and there can be a blessed and merciful stopper that the person may not realize.

50. The Ant and the Carpet

There was a Sufi in the mosque. She saw an ant walking on the carpet. The carpet was nice and green with some designs. The Sufi said to herself, "Wow! This ant probably thinks that he is in a green ocean."

In the above story, the ant was on a two-dimensional plane compared to the Sufi with a three-dimensional plane who can see the design of the carpet. The Sufi was above the carpet, looking down. In practice, it is understood and experienced that there can be millions of dimensions. Some mystics can experience some of them.

Similarly, the knowledge and experiences of the Transcendent, the High, God can sometimes be simplified and reduced to the human understandings of time and space. One should not forget that the similarities do not give the person the essence about the Divine. There is always room for error. Therefore, caution with possibilities and the statement of "God knows the best" is added in internal and external expressions.

The ant on the green carpet

51. Sufi and the Right Answer

There was a Sufi in the mosque. A man with inflexible beliefs came and wanted to do some missionary work. He wanted the Sufi to go with him. The Sufi did not want to go but he said to himself, "If I say that I don't want to go, he will argue with me and I don't want to waste my time." He said to the man "I will think about it . . . " The man left the Sufi alone.

It is always important to reflect and think well before uttering any words to any person. Therefore, Sufis prefer silence and purposeful talking if and when necessary. If they are put in a difficult situation of choice they try to use wisdom to minimize any evil and undesired effects.

52. Sufi and Choosing His Prospective Wife

There were two single Sufis who wanted to get married. They heard that there is a girl who wants to get married as well. The first Sufi who got the news said to himself, "I should not be selfish. I should have my friend first consider marrying her." He went and told his Sufi friend. His friend was not interested and he already had arrangements for another girl. The first Sufi said to himself, "OK, then maybe I should meet with this girl." Then, he happened to see this girl in the mosque and shocked, said to himself, "I will never get married with this girl. She is so ugly." A few years passed. He married this girl. After he had kids from this girl, he remembered his promise not to get married with this girl and he blamed himself and said, "My negative thoughts about others."

Sometimes, in practice, the person can be tested with the things that he or she does not want. Therefore, the Sufis try to catch their bad thoughts before the opposite happens. This is a level in which the Sufis try to watch and be conscious about their thoughts.

53. Sufi and Not Flying

There was a Sufi man who went to the airport to take his brother who was flying to England. As his brother was going to the plane, he waved to his brother and said to himself, "I will never fly to England. It is such an ugly country." After a few years, he went to England and he liked it so much. He said to himself, "I should not have those thoughts in my mind."

In the above history, the Sufi did not want to fly to England and had some negative thoughts about it. God made him fly there in order to rectify his thoughts about different places and people.

54. Sufi and Burping

There was a Sufi in the mosque. He heard an old lady burping constantly and she could not control herself. Sufi had a feeling of disgust. Immediately, he caught and stopped his thoughts and feelings and said, "Astagfirullah."

In the above story, the Sufi was afraid that if he did not catch his negative thoughts and feelings about the situation of the old lady, he would face the same problem when he became old or sooner. In practice, a person can have instant negative feelings and thoughts toward others. Those are not harmful as long as they don't become permanent and they are terminated with certain mindful chants such as "Astagfirullah" which means, "Oh God, forgive me for my bad thoughts about others."

55. King and the Sufi

A king one day asks every inhabitant of his kingdom what they want. Everyone wants something different. Someone asks for pounds of gold. Another person asks for a lot of land with many fruit trees. A person asks for a number of cows, sheep, and chickens. A Sufi comes and asks for the king himself and the king is startled and asks, "Why do you want me?" He responds, "If I have you, whatever you own is mine." In Sufi tradition, the highest intention to perform chants, rituals, or service to other people is the pleasure of God. If one pleases God, God can give boundless rewards and pleasure from the Mighty Kingdom.

In Sufi tradition, the highest intention to perform chants, rituals, or service to other people is the pleasure of God. If one pleases God, God can give boundless rewards and pleasure from the Mighty Kingdom.

56. Sufi, Change, and God

One day a Sufi saw her old friend with another person that she had not seen for a few years. After the greetings, her old friend started introducing her. The Sufi was a little bit uncomfortable because the Sufi was not the same Sufi that her friend used to know a few years ago. Every hour he was different.

In Sufism, change and advancement on the spiritual path is good. Every day a person is expected to go further in the closeness and union with God. The only unchanged One is God. God's attributes are constant and unchanged—the difference between the creation and Creator.

57. Sufi and the Preface of a Book

There was a Sufi who bought a new book on spiritual advancement written by a famous teacher. The book was translated to English. The translator was a Sufi as well and also a student of the teacher. The translator wrote in the preface a very harsh critique for the ones criticizing the book without genuine intention and learning. The Sufi was shocked with this type of introduction in the preface. The Sufi was upset about it.

The Sufi books are generally written for the ones who have sincere intention to learn and sympathize with the travelers. In practice, the traditional followers, simple intellectuals, or people with the diseases of the heart such as jealousy and arrogance may not be able to benefit from these writings unless there is a sincere intention.

58. Sufi and the Satan

One day the Sufi was praying at night in her home. Satan approached her to distract her from her engagement in prayer. After finishing the prayer, she said to Satan: "Why don't you make repentance? God's mercy is infinite." Satan said: "No, I will prove that I am right."

Sometimes, intellectual discourses prevent the person from genuine learning due to the disease of "I will prove that I am right." In the scripture, one of the traits of a person is accepting the good, beautiful, and truthful whenever and whoever it comes from.[8] Then, God makes everything easy for that person.

---

8. Surah layl ... (SaddaqabilHusna).

59. Sufi and the Handyman

There was a Sufi and a drunk, poor handyman. Sufi was trying to help him by giving him some work at his house and advising him on changing his bad and destructive habits. The handyman was coming to the Sufi's home. One day, the Sufi gave him a small loan so that the handyman could buy a car and not be dependent on people, because with gambling and drinking he had lost everything. Then, the Sufi saw a dream the same night that the handyman's face was turned into a fox and was snickering and smiling. The Sufi woke up and didn't understand what the dream meant. Then, he called the handyman, but he didn't answer. One call, two, three, many calls, no answer . . . Next day, next month, no answer from the handyman. The Sufi was worried about the handyman. He said to himself, "I hope he is OK. I don't care about the loan." Then, finally, he reached one of his friends. His friend said he left town and will not come back again. The Sufi said, "Alhamdulillah, he is OK."

In Sufism, thinking good about people is the key even though the people may have bad traits. In the above story, it seems that the handyman intended to leave the town without paying the Sufi. Therefore, he seemed to trick the Sufi as shown within his dream interpretation. Although the Sufi might have understood the meaning of his dream, still he was worried about the handyman, not his money.

60. The Sufi and the Questions

There was a Sufi in the mosque. He used to answer everyone's questions. The people used to observe of him that depending on the person, he used to give different answers to each person. He was asked the reason. He said, "Everyone has a different understanding level. It is not what you say but how they understand it."

The prophet[9] used to give short answers to desert travelers appropriate to their understanding. He used to implement the notion that everyone in practice has a different level. Recognizing this is important. Not everyone can be intellectuals. Not everyone can be devout but may want to know what is sufficient. Therefore, all the struggles are valuable to God.

---

9. Iyad, Qadi. 2006. *Ash-Shifa*. Madina Press.

61. The Funny Handyman and the Sufi

There was a funny handyman. He was making a joke that people always say Alhamdullillah (thank you God) but then complain. They say InshAllah (if God wills) but then they don't follow what they say. Sufi started smiling . . .

In practice, expressions have meanings. If the people don't follow what they say it is not the problem of expression but the problem of the person. "Alhamdullillah" (thanks be to God) is an expression to remind the person not to complain but to always be appreciative. When this is chanted it has an effect on the heart and mind. When the person says "InshAllah" it is a reminder that the real power is from God.

62. Sufi and the Deaf Man

There was a deaf person in the mosque. The Sufi was good friends with him. The Sufi knew sign language and talked to him. Everyone in the mosque used to feel bad for the deaf person that he couldn't hear or talk. The deaf person told the Sufi that he feels bad for these people. They waste their time, minds, and hearts in nonsense talk. The deaf person used to express gratitude to God that he can't talk. He was always in the peaceful state of silence.

Silence is one of the desired states in the practice. A person who talks most of the time does not listen. He or she may think that the person understands, but not really. Real understanding and embodiment comes with experience, reflection, and personalization in the practice. Statistically speaking, a person who talks a lot can make more errors and can break more hearts than others. God knows the best, as Sufis avow.

63. Sufi Teacher and the Kids

There was a teacher in the mosque who used to teach the kids. After shouting at the kids, he used to give candies. Although the teacher seemed to be angry and shouting to an outsider, the kids seemed to love him. He used to smile also and explain the lecture well. Kids seemed to interpret the teacher's treatment not as abuse or hate, but as a method of teaching. The kids felt this genuine intention and feelings from the teacher. Sufi was watching this and said to herself, "Wow, this is similar to the relationship between the person and God."

In the practice, God does not get angry like humans. Anger in humans can be a deficient quality. God gives opportunities and learning experiences to people to excel in the path of perfecting their relationship with the Divine. It is up to the person to take heed from each experience as a self-learning opportunity to build a positive relationship with God.

64. Sufi and the Literalist

One day, the Sufi was sitting in the mosque. A literalist was teaching the knowledge of God to the children. Sufi was listening and impressed. He said to himself, "Wow, one should learn the initial knowledge of God without any interpretation from a literalist. Then, the person can learn the interpretation from the Sufis."

In normative Sufism, it is very important to learn the religious laws as some people call them as literalist because they avoid interpretation. Legal laws or literal approach is the cloth and frame of the meanings. Without these pillars, the foundation can collapse. Therefore, a good Sufi in practice can be a good expert in legal or literal teachings of the religion.

65. Sufi and Different Languages

There was a Sufi who knew a few languages. He used to enjoy scriptures and saintly writings in their original language. He used to also look at different translations of the same text in different languages to get genuine, culturally embedded meanings. He was trying to understand and personalize the concepts in words in each language in order to reach their intended meanings.

In practice, it is very critical and encouraged to chant and practice the divine phrases in their original language of revelation. Although the person may not be a native speaker of that language, the divine sounds have effects on the heart and mind without even understanding the meanings, according to the practice. When the person puts forth an effort to learn the meanings of the phrases, then the effects of spiritual engagement can increase.

66. Sufi and Her Book

One day a Sufi wrote a book. She was invited to teach people from her book. She was explaining and having the students write reflection papers on each chapter. Next class, she was listening to the students about what they understood. She was getting great pleasure from it.

Similarly, one of the notions in the practice is that God created the universe to have the divine attributes and names to be known. The natural sciences and other sciences in our modern life can reflect the different names and attributes of God in practice. God is pleased when a person puts forth an effort to increase his or her knowledge of God. In other words, reading the book of the universe, the human self, and scriptures can increase one's knowledge in the path of God and God can be pleased about it.

67. Sufi and Phrases on the Tongue

There was a Sufi who used to memorize divine phrases and parts of the Quran in their original language of revelation. She was trying to understand the meanings but sometimes she did not understand the meanings, and yet still memorized it. One day, she was sleeping and woke up with one of the words that she had memorized, and found that she was repeating it involuntarily. She looked up the meaning of the word that she was repeating and said to herself, "Aha! That is the answer. Now everything makes sense."

In practice, divine phrases and verses from the scripture can embody different beings and can help the person in different parts of life difficulties. When the person appreciates God and all the divine phrases and the scripture from God, they can act like a superman to save the person in the times of need. It is kind of a payback time. When the person needs help, they come. This is a common belief across the tradition. Each phrase, chant, prayer, and recitation of the scripture can take different forms to help the person in this world and in the afterlife. There are narrations that the five times prayers of a person can come in the form of a human being after the person's death in the grave or on the judgment day and can comfort the person from all worries. When the person sees this unknown person the person asks, "Who are you?" and this unknown person replies, "I am your prayers that you used to pray. Now, it is my turn to help you."

68. Sufi and the Huffing and Puffing Handyman

There was a Sufi hiding in the mosque. He did not want people to know where he was in the mosque and he did not want to be bothered. He wanted to enjoy his readings, chanting, and coffee. One day, someone opened the door and Sufi was not looking. The man started praying and making a noise of huffing and puffing while he was praying. The Sufi said to himself, "It should be the old handyman" and it was.

Huffing and puffing sounds of a person outside a prayer can mean complaints, negativity, or depression. When a person has these genuine sounds of huffing and puffing in a prayer this can mean charge and discharge or empty and fill effects, while one is re-establishing a connection with God. Therefore, when huffing and puffing sincerely and involuntarily comes in one's prayer, it can show a very high value of genuine connection of the person with God.

69. The Lucky Sufi

There was a Sufi who used to rent a house. His rich landlord loved him so much. One day, his landlord died and he left a will for the Sufi that the Sufi will inherit the house. When the Sufi heard this, he said, "Alhamdullillah, and this is exactly me and my Lord."

In practice, the life is rented by God to the person. Then, God treats the person as if he/she owns her own life with free will and free choice. As a tenant of his or her house of body and soul, the person comes from nowhere as the owner of it and acts accordingly. Finally, the fake landlord sells the house to the Real Lord with a business transaction of recognition and appreciation of God. In the scripture, the Quran, this notion of business transaction between the person and God is mentioned in multiple places [57:11].

70. Sufi and the Magic

There was a Sufi who used to give lectures. One day there were a few new people who attended the lectures and made magic on the Sufi to see if she was really a genuine teacher. The Sufi understood this. She protected herself with the divine phrases from the effects of this evil attempt. She said to herself, "I feel bad for these people, instead of focusing on their own selves and benefiting from the lectures and group chants, they are trying to harm others."

In practice, magic has an effect on the people but it is considered lowly and a great sin to perform magic. Sufis learn the necessary tools, chants, and phrases to protect themselves from the evil talismanic effects. Ultimately, they firmly believe that the effect is created by God. By taking refuge in God, these attempts may have only temporary effects if any. On the other hand, the person involved in any type of evil, including magic, that person harms herself or himself before harming others. In the above story, although the people may have good intention to test the teacher's authenticity, it is considered evil to use magic to harm the Sufi. In other words, to achieve a good outcome or result, all the means to reach that goal should also be good. For example, one cannot steal money and help the poor. Stealing is evil and helping is good. Good and evil do not mix.

71. Milk, Pee, and the Sufi

There was a student who did not understand the concept of mixing good and bad in spiritual and ethical teachings on the path. He came to the Sufi and asked this question. The student used to like and drink fresh milk. The Sufi took a bottle of fresh organic milk and he took a drop of pee from the restroom and put it inside the bottle in front of the student. Then, the Sufi gave the bottle to the student and said, "Why don't you drink it? It's fresh milk." The student was disgusted and he was not able to drink it. The Sufi said, "Are you sure? It is all nice, organic fresh milk. There is just a tiny amount, less than 0.01% pee." The student smiled and said, "I understood."

In practice, all the virtuous goals should be achieved by virtuous spiritual acts and intentions. A person cannot purposefully do evil and expect a good outcome. Even though the outcome may look good, God ultimately considers genuine intentions and efforts in connection with pure and sincere struggles. In the above story, the student did not drink the milk due to the impurity although it was a minuscule amount.

72. Rotation of the Days and the Sufi

There was a Sufi in the mosque. An old man came and said that his car was stolen. The Sufi was trying to help the person to call the police. The Sufi felt bad for the old man. Then, the Sufi went to his home. His wife said that her best friend's sister is dying due to pancreatic cancer. The Sufi was sad and prayed for her. Then, the Sufi got sick and was admitted to the emergency room. The Sufi thought about all these recent incidents and smiled to himself, "Rotation of the days."

In Sufism, God rotates evil or good-looking days among people to reveal the real character of the people. Below is a passage from the Quran that alludes to this notion [3:149].

> If an evil touched you
> Then remember that
> Evil touches others as well.
>
> These are the days
> We rotate among the people
> Good and evil
>
> So that the real characters
> Of people are revealed
> God knows it and
> You become witness to it as well
>
> Remember God does not like oppressors.

One of the states in practice is the station of patience. When an evil hits the person, if the person does not complain but still appreciates what comes from God, then the person can use this as an opportunity to excel spiritually. Although in practice, everyone asks for good and an easy life, if for some reason it does not happen, the notion of patience is practiced. In both good and evil-looking days, the person appreciates the relationship with God.

73. Sufi and Her Book

One day, a Sufi wrote a book about inner spiritual states and said to herself, "Wow, if a person reads this book they will be immersed in it." As the time passed and she observed the people, they did not give the proper attention to the book that the Sufi had originally expected. She now told herself, "Now, I understand. There is an original Book from God; people don't care and are heedless. If it is a human's book, it is normal."

In practice, heedlessness, or being in the state of "not caring" can be the attitude of many toward prophets, miracles, scriptures, and genuine writings of the spiritual path. It is most of the time not the fault of the text or messenger but the receiver or the audience. In physics, to decode the signals from a sender, the receiver should be able to decode the incoming wavelengths with the same frequency.

74. Sufi and Two Cases

There was a Sufi looking from the window. While looking at the window, she saw two people. One person was addicted to drugs and trying to terrorize people to get money. Another person was walking and seeing an old woman, wanting to help her with her stuff and carry her bags to the station. The Sufi was thinking to try to understand these two cases.

In Sufism, external representations reflect internal states. In a human being, there is good, love, humbleness. At the same time, there are evil, anger, and arrogance. The person has a choice, free will, but is accountable for one's decision. The person has a goal on the path to excel in the betterment of oneself. If the person does not practice or exercise following a path, or rituals, then the person can be in duality in the inner self struggles, in choosing right or wrong.

A human's inner self is like a huge system of government. If the person has the systems or institutions to govern and implement with law enforcement through rituals, then a healthy government or society is constructed. This is called a self on the journey in practice. Therefore, in the above story, there are two different selves involved in making a decision and acting on it.

75. Third World Countries and the Sufi

There was a Sufi helping some refugees in the shelter house. While she was leaving the shelter house, an American friend of the Sufi approached her and told her, "I feel bad for these refugees. They come from third world countries, with raw conditions." The Sufi smiled and said, "I feel worse about the third world selves than the ones from the third world countries."

In practice, there is the initial level of raw selves. This self is not trained, can enjoy the evil and prevent the good. The second level of self does recognize one's mistakes and feels sorry about it. The third level of self is the best, knows oneself and God, knows the good and the evil, acts on it, and intends to please God. The Sufi in the above story has categorized the self, according to the internal conditions of the person rather than the external ones.

76. Communication with the Unknowns and Unseen

There was a Sufi who used to engage with people in different religious traditions. She was really surprised when people were getting scared about the unknowns and unseen especially related to the ones after death. She really felt bad about them but was not able to do anything except give them some advice about believing in the Creator and practicing the rituals.

In practice, depending on the level of the person, there are really no unknowns and unseen. An advanced person on the path can experience God, angels, the good and evil doers, the authentic versus non-authentic, and all others with certainty. Death is a wrong word according to the Sufis. Death is only a removal of the barriers for the layman. For a Sufi, death is nothing newer than having temporary states becoming permanent stations. In the journey of ascension, the Prophet visited different dimensions of unseen and unknowns such as the various conditions and dwelling places of the people after death. One of the lowest states in spiritual advancement is the cognition of the condition of the people in the graveyard.

77. The Sufi and the Pancreatic Cancer

There was a Sufi. Her friend's sister became ill and diagnosed with pancreatic cancer. She was thirty-eight years old with a few kids and a crying husband. Everyone was visiting her in the hospital. A few days were left before her expected departure day from the world. Finally, she died and everyone was crying. The friends made some food for the family. The funeral ended and the deceased was sent to the cemetery. The Sufi visited her friend. She was still crying. The Sufi said: "We will meet them soon. They just left a little bit early before us."

In practice, although death can look ugly, it ends the pains for the ones who are always missing God. In practice, tribulations and tests are given to the people to increase their spiritual level before meeting with God as long as there are no complaints in the relationship with the Divine. One can welcome the evil-looking incidents if one is constantly engaged in regular prayers, rituals, and reading the scripture. These daily practices are called wird or awrad, the daily spiritual regular practices.

78. Sufi and Her Teacher

There was a Sufi who did not see her teacher for a long time. She really missed her and left her home to drive eleven hours to visit her teacher. Her teacher always had guests visiting from different places. This time, it was not many but perhaps only sixty to seventy people. The teacher was giving a lecture. The Sufi sat down. The teacher from nowhere started explaining about the importance of using every second of time meaningfully and mindfully in the spiritual advancement in the relationship with the Divine. The teacher discussed spiritual arrogance and the difficulties on the path. The Sufi said to herself, "Alhamdullillah, I got what I needed. Thank you, Allah." Then, she left to drive another eleven hours to reach her home.

In practice, the genuine teachers know and are aware of the students' need and accordingly they escort them on the spiritual path. It is not uncommon in practice for the people to visit a teacher for a short period of time after traveling hours and days, and then going back to their homes. A few minutes, an hour, a day can be sufficient to charge the person spiritually and then she or he can go back home. The presence of the teacher or the place can have an effect on the seeker depending on the sincere intention and the struggle of the person.

79. The Rich Sufi and His Teacher's Food

One day, there was a rich Sufi. He was not feeling well. He wanted to visit his teacher to be in his presence. He went and visited him. He felt better and was waiting for dinnertime to come in order to eat the food prepared in the Sufi center where his teacher resided. For dinner, as usual, there was soup and salad. The Sufi ate and felt much better and left the center.

In practice, there is a blessing in eating from the food prepared in the place where the teacher resides. Due to a high level of spiritual presence, chants, and prayers, it is believed that the food has a curing effect of physical and spiritual diseases. In the above story, the Sufi was rich and he could have eaten a better food but he waited to eat a simpler but blessed food prepared at the Sufi center where his teacher resided.

80. The Teacher and Humbleness

One day, the Sufi visited her teacher. The teacher was giving a lecture and using some harsh words against herself to humiliate her own ego in front of the public. The Sufi was listening and trying to take a lesson from the lecture for her own self.

In practice, the teachers are humans. Although the teachers are spiritually blessed and the students revere them so much, they see and locate themselves at the lowest level in order to not be trapped with spiritual arrogance. Genuine humbleness and humility of the teacher is one of the character traits of a good teacher.

81. Sufi and the Hindu

There was a Sufi. He had a good friend who was a Hindu. They were discussing life after death. His Hindu friend mentioned their belief of reincarnation. The Sufi was thinking. He said, "When there are different species, if they mix, there may be abnormalities or exceptions. One may not base a general rule on exceptions or abnormalities." The Hindu friend was thinking... The Sufi continued: "In the scriptures such as the Bible, Torah, or Quran, God mentions explicitly about the Divine Self and about the unknowns after death." Sufi wanted to know the source of the afterlife belief in his friend's tradition and said: "Is reincarnation a logical deduction? Is it an interpretation from your scripture?" The Hindu was thinking.

In Sufi practice, the logic should not contradict with the belief. Below is a methodology that the Sufis follow when learning from different sources of divine knowledge related to the known, the unknown, and the unseen:

1. The first source of knowledge is knowing God through God. In other words, how God explains the Divine Self in the scriptures.
2. Knowing God through the interpretations of the prophets and messengers of God.
3. Knowing God through the intellect (reason).
4. Knowing God through the interpretation of the saints.
5. Learning through conscience (sixth sense).
6. Having the experience at any stage during the learning process to confirm or triangulate the sources from one to five.

82. Sufi and the Safety

Sufi had a Christian friend. They were talking about the understanding of being saved in this world and the afterlife. His friend said, "If the person has correct belief, then the person can be saved." Then, the Sufi added, "I agree, that is a possibility but not a certainty until the person dies."

In practice, if the person has the right belief and good action, the person can be saved from punishment and be rewarded. However, although this is all highly likely, it is not for sure. The notion is that the person does not really know the reality of his or her intention or sincerity in performing good actions. Therefore, there are a lot of stories in the tradition of people who were worshippers of God but thrown to hellfire as a result of showing off, or for trying to attract worldly gains and benefits. Conversely, there are stories about the people who were in external disobedience to God and died and were forgiven by God due to their internal sincere intention. Although there is a general rule in the scriptures that people who have the right belief and action can be saved, Sufism still maintains some uncertainty due to not fully knowing one's inner self. This notion of uncertainty always keeps the traveler spiritually alert and self-accountable in the relationship with humans and God.

83. Sufi and the Escort

One day a Sufi was looking at the window. He saw an escort truck carrying money from the bank. There were a few armed men protecting the truck. The Sufi saw this scene and in amazement said, "Wow, this is exactly the belief[10] of the person. It needs more escort."

In practice, the right belief is very valuable and needs to be escorted. Therefore, when one is learning about God and the rules of the path, the originality and authenticity is vital. Choosing an authentic path, studying with a good and genuine teacher, and following these priceless guidelines are the key. Once the person starts the journey and builds up the core values of the relationship with the Divine, then this treasure and diamond should be escorted. This diamond cannot be put at risk by any inauthentic knowledge, teacher, or experience. The person should know the skills of letting in and blocking out so that the treasure can increase without being infected with the diseases.

Escorting the valuables

---

10. Iman.

84. Firefighters, Roof Rats, and the Sufis

There were two Sufis. One was American and the other was from overseas. They were walking and they saw a fire truck that was going on a rescue mission. On the fire truck, it was written "roof rats." The Sufi from overseas asked the American Sufi why it was written "roof rats." The American Sufi said the firefighters praise that they can climb on the roof like a rat. The Sufi from overseas smiled and said, "If you call someone a rat in our country, it is a curse, not a praise."

Sometimes, language has its contextual meanings depending on the culture. In the above story, a word at a wrong time and place can mean a curse or praise. In practice, it is essential to learn the etiquette of the spiritual behaviors in relation to the different contexts and people. This is called adab. It is especially important to learn the etiquette related to the teachers, lecturers, and other peers. It ultimately helps to establish a relationship with God with the notions of adab.

85. The Rich Sufi, Online Shopping, and the Poor Sufi

One day a poor Sufi visited the rich Sufi. She saw that her friend was shopping online although it was expensive. The poor Sufi said, "Why don't you shop in the store so that you can save some money and help the poor with what you saved?" The rich Sufi said, "I don't have time. My time is valuable. If I have some extra time, I would spend it in chanting and prayers rather than going to the store and shopping."

In practice, both approaches are acceptable as long as the person has the right intention. It is important not to assume or judge people externally but to always have good thoughts for other fellows.

86. Sufi and Temporary Things

One day, a Sufi missed his wife very much. He went home to see her but did not receive much attention from her. Then, he left his home. Next day, he missed his daughter and went home to see her. His daughter did not care that he came home and the Sufi was disappointed. Then, he left his home. Next day, he missed his friends that he used to hang around. He went to visit his friends. His friends were in their own world and the Sufi felt disconnected from them. Then, he left them. Finally, he decided to visit the places where he was born and where he had spent all of his childhood years. He went there and found that everything looked different and he felt so isolated and deeply in pain. At the end, he understood that he needs to travel to the internal house.

In Sufi writings, the house generally symbolizes the heart where the person has a close relationship with God. In the above story, the Sufi was disappointed with the temporary friends. At the end, he turned to the permanent, real, appreciative, and understanding Friend—God. In practice, it is believed that everything can be a cause of pain except God. Everything can include all of one's loved ones, friends, and family members. A Sufi among loved ones can be lonely. A Sufi in prison can be happy, enjoying all pleasures.

87. Sufi Teacher and the Clock

One day a Sufi visited her teacher. There were twenty to thirty people sitting in a small room with the teacher. Everyone was sitting in this gathering in silence. There was only the chirping sound of the seconds of a clock in the room. This clock was an interesting one. In each second, a page was turning in this clock that looked like a book. The Sufi was thinking, and enjoying the silence and presence of the gathering and the teacher.

In the above story, it is a common practice to sit in silence next to the teacher for a few minutes, maybe more. The effect of the presence of good and spiritual people has an effect on the person's heart and mind. Instead of a formal lecture, there was a silent lecture in the above story. The notion of presence of the teacher and the silent lecture is a term that is used in practice to emphasize the effect of being with good and genuinely spiritual people and teachers.[11] Also, a turning page in a book-looking clock can signify the importance of each second of time for advancement in the spiritual journey in relationship with the Divine. Some Sufis believe that if a second is equal to a passed second in the experience and knowledge of God, then that can be a loss.[12]

---

11. This is called tawajjuh of the teacher on the students. Tawajjuh are the inspirations of the teacher to the students in order to teach, elevate them spiritually, or protect them from evil.
12. The Prophet mentions that a believer is in loss if one's day is equal to a previous day in closeness to God and that there should be a constant advancement on the path.

88. Sufi and Perception

There was a Sufi who was not rich and not poor. She had a middle income. Each time she had a desire to eat from an expensive restaurant she said, "I mentally assume that I went to that restaurant. I ate a nice food and a nice dessert." After enjoying this mentally, she ate her normal, simple food at home and put the saved money in a box that she was planning to use to go to the restaurant. Later, she had an urge to buy an expensive car. She saved a good amount of money. Then, she bought a normal, simple car. Each time she was using her simple car she was assuming that her car was the most expensive car. She put the remaining money in a box that she was planning to use to buy the expensive car. Over the course of years, her savings accumulated and she used that money to build a mosque for the people to worship in and for the homeless to find shelter. The name of the mosque was called "Assumption."[13]

In Sufi practice, the training of the self or ego is very important. The raw self is generally similar to a naughty child. He may ask a lot of things, beneficial or harmful. A parent does not give to the child exactly what he wants but gives in proportion with wisdom. If the child gets what he wants there may not be teaching or self-training or behavioral development. Similarly, a person should know one's self well and accordingly apply different treatment methods.

---

13. There is a real mosque in Istanbul, Turkey, with that name due to the story mentioned above.

89. Now I Understood! and the Sufi

There was a Sufi who did not understand why she was sometimes in spiritual pain and sometimes not. She was engaging in prayer, chanting, reading the scripture, going to mosque, and feeling good; but sometimes when she was not engaged she was feeling so much pain, detachment, and loneliness. One day, she was traveling on a plane. She was thinking again about the painful moments of detachment, disconnection, loneliness, and physical torture. During her trip, she was constantly engaged in chanting with her beads, reading her scripture, and learning from her sacred prophetic books. She was feeling so happy. She was looking down while walking and not looking around at the people and not engaging with her surroundings. As the moments of happiness continued, she said, "Alhamdulillah, now I have understood!"

In the above story, the Sufi was in pain when she was detached from God and not engaged in any type of mental, verbal, or physical ritual. In one of the narrations from the Prophet, the highest level of angel—Gabriel—comes, visits him, and teaches him that the highest level of spiritual pleasure, engagement, and happiness is removing yourself and your ego every time it blocks your spiritual progress and causes pain striving to always be in the state of Union.[14]

---

14. Ihsan.

90. The Level of Union and the Evil

As the Sufi was enjoying the station of union with the Divine, she went to visit some old friends. She took the bus, and then the train, and finally reached their home. She rang the bell three times but no one answered the door. They were supposed to be home. The Sufi did not get angry and left a small gift at their door with a note. She smiled and left to go to the bus station for her appointment. The application on her phone showed her that the bus was coming soon—in two minutes. Two minutes, three minutes, five minutes, ten minutes, there was no bus . . . She smiled and called the Uber and finally made it to her appointment.

In the story above, the Sufi still experienced some type of annoying or evil-looking incidents but she did not perceive them as evil and she moved on. Her level of union with the Divine changed her perception, making her calm and peaceful when she encountered the evil.

91. The Uber Driver, Cursing, and the Coffee

As the Sufi was late to her appointment, she called Uber to get there instead of taking the bus. A nice Uber car came and picked up the Sufi. The driver was so nice and the Sufi was enjoying the ride. Then, there was a car which abruptly cut off the road in front of this Uber car. The Uber driver started cursing the other car and he became so disturbed. The Sufi was watching the scene and trying to get a meaning from it. They finally reached their destination. While the Sufi was leaving the car, she forgot her coffee in the car. The driver called the Sufi and said, "You forgot your coffee. That is the most important thing." The Sufi smiled and then said to herself, "This is the reason why the driver was so disturbed. There is no Union."

In practice, a person's real spiritual state can reveal itself at the encounters of different evil-looking incidents. In the above story, although the driver seemed very nice in the beginning, he lost his temper in a very small evil-looking incident. When he mentioned that "the coffee is the most important thing," then the Sufi interpreted that the driver's short temperament is due to his engagement with temporal things such as coffee. A person in practice gets real empowerment from the permanent One, God, on the journey.

The peaceful Uber driver losing his temper

92. The Crying Boy and the Sufi

There was a Sufi. He saw a father and a son. The boy was crying for something futile. The father was looking at him and he was feeling bad for his son. The father did not give what the boy wanted. The boy was still crying and trying to get the attention of the father. At the end, the father taught a lesson to his son and gave him better than what he wanted and the son was so happy. The Sufi was looking at the scene and said, "SubhanAllah, that is the relation between Allah and a person."

In Sufi practice, a person prays[15] constantly, cries, and asks. It may be that the person is asking for something futile, useless, or harmful. During the time of asking and crying through prayer, the person can feel pain and neglected. Sometimes, she may even think, "Why are my prayers not being accepted?" The One, who is always Active, Hearing, and Merciful appreciates the effort and sincere humbleness of the person in relationship with the Creator. At the end, due to these efforts, God can give the person better than what is asked for, although the person may not initially understand this.

The Sufi father helping his son with his broken toy

---

15. Dua in Ar.

93. The Huffing and Puffing Man and the Sufi

There was a man who used to come to the mosque and pray. He used to constantly come and tell his problems to the Sufi. This man used to complain about his family members and other people, claiming that everyone was always unjust to him. If the Sufi wanted to give him some advice, he did not want to listen—only talk and blame others. One day, the Sufi was in the mosque studying. This man came and he was huffing and puffing. He saw the Sufi studying and did not want to disturb him. Sufi understood the case and prolonged his studying in order to not be disturbed. The man was pacing back and forth in the mosque, huffing and puffing, waiting and peering in on the Sufi to find out if he finished his studying so that he could talk to him as usual. Five minutes, ten minutes, half an hour, one hour . . . the Sufi was still studying. His head was in the book and the man was circulating within the mosque, huffing and puffing and checking if the Sufi had finished his studying. The Sufi smiled and said to himself, "I know you want to talk to me but I know I can't help you until you sit down and engage yourself with reading the scripture, engage in prayer and chanting, and do some self-reflection. Then your problems will be solved."

In practice, humans really don't solve any problems. Even their apathy and lack of concern about one's problem can add more pain to the person's suffering. The real helper, listener, and concerned is only One, God. Although the person may think that no one is hearing or talking back, the mystical answers from God can be revealed to the person whether the person understands or not.

94. Sufi, Cat, and the Natural Habitat

One day a Sufi visited a friend of hers in America. Her friend had an indoor cat. The Sufi was surprised that the cats were kept at home and they were not allowed to go outside. Each morning when the Sufi woke up, she saw that the cats were rushing to the window to look outside as her friend was opening the blinds. One day, the Sufi said to her friend, "Can I please take them into the backyard for a few minutes? I feel that it is their natural habitat. I feel bad for them as they rush every morning to look out the window." Her friend said, "Okay." The Sufi opened the glass door from the house to the backyard. The cats came to the edge of the door and they were scared to go outside and they didn't go. The Sufi was thinking . . . and finally she smiled and said, "This is exactly the relationship between the person and God. The cats need time."

In Sufism, it is the human's genuine nature[16] to establish a relationship with God. In a pure human self, a person can feel this desire and needs it fully. As the person grows, if the person moves away from his or her pure self, an artificial, trained self can replace that in the person. Then, abnormal can become normal. Unnatural can become natural. In the above story, since the cats were domesticated to stay at home, they felt that something was pulling them to their natural habitat. Therefore, they rushed every day to observe the sun, plants, and other beings from the window of the house. In this new self of the cats, when they were invited to go to their natural habitat they were scared. The Sufi said, "The cats need time" to indicate that to transform from unnatural to natural, it can take time but it is possible. One can always re-establish a natural relationship with one's own pure self and God but it can require time, sincere effort, and good teachers.

The cat longing for the nature

---

16. This is called fitrah.

95. Rain Drops and the Sufi

One day, there was a physicist Sufi. She was sitting under a tree and thinking about the gravitational force. Then, while she was in deep reflection, it started raining. The Sufi said to herself, "Wow, SubhanAllah! The raindrops are not touching each other and they are not falling with a fully accelerated speed that could make a hole in my head. It is all mercy and gratitude from God."

Sufis often reflect upon nature, the natural phenomena, and about their inspirations in relation to the different names and attributes of God. In the above story, the physicist Sufi was amazed with each raindrop because they were repelling each other but not gushing as if they were pouring from a hose. She was also amazed with the fact that the raindrops fell with a final,[17] non-harmful speed upon the earth, as one normally can expect a huge speed due to the acceleration from the distance of thousands of feet.

---

17. This speed is called final velocity in physics.

96. Focused Eating and the Sufi

There was a rich Sufi who used to only eat one type of food in each meal and enjoyed it a lot. A friend of hers asked her what the reason was for her practice. She said: "When I have a variety of food on the table I cannot focus on the taste of each one. I may just take a bite from each to be respectful if someone brings or serves, but I generally focus on one type of food."

In spiritual practices, it is important to focus on one path and become an expert, and then wander to taste others when there is an opportunity. In chanting, prayers, and meditation, the notion of repetition with one phrase can give the same approach of focus on taste through charge and discharge. The overall notion of believing in One Creator alludes to the notion that simplicity with focus is for everyone and that this approach is genuine, pure, and natural.

There are places to recognize complexity and there are places to recognize simplicity. Correct recognition in different contexts can help the spiritual traveler to benefit from it on the journey. Misplacements can distract and sometimes even take the person away from a genuine path.

97. The Nice Flower and the Eye

One day, a Sufi brought a nice tulip flower to the mosque. She was enjoying it by looking at it while staying and praying in this temple. Every Friday, hundreds of people came to the mosque and prayed there. She used to take the tulip to her house in order to not show it to the hundreds of people. One day, she was traveling and forgot to take the tulip to her home. She came the next day and cried out, "My tulip, the evil eye." The Sufi was very sad.

In practice, the effect of the eye on living things is an expected phenomenon. Therefore, if a person likes something or is astonished, one should say "MashAllah" to remove the effect of the evil eye. MashAllah can translate as "What a great creation of God." In the above story, there were a lot of people who came to the mosque and probably liked the tulip. Maybe they didn't say the word "MashAllah," and the tulip was affected by the eye and died.

98. The Marriage Problem and the Sufi

There was a man who used to have marital problems with his wife. He wanted to meet with the Sufi to get some advice. They went to a coffee shop. The man started talking for almost half an hour that his expectations were not fulfilled and that he was so disappointed with her. Finally, the man stopped talking. The Sufi said, "Are you done?" The man replied, "Yes." The Sufi said, "My only advice to you is: Don't make your expectations too high!" The man said, "Yes, you are right," and he kept saying, "I made my expectations too high . . . " and left the coffee shop repeating this phrase.

In Sufi practice, humans are humans. They have their own limitations. If a person submits or surrenders to a human being instead of God, there will be frustrations and disappointments. If a husband sees his wife as perfect or vice versa, if a person views a friend as perfect, or if a child sees a parent as perfect, then they will definitely face frustrations. The only one to whom one can fully turn with full submission and surrender and with expectations of perfection is God. Most of the time, people's fake replacements of God with others puts people in jeopardy, stress, disappointment, and frustration. It is encouraged to always have positive and high expectations from God. If the person becomes frustrated in the relationship with God as well, then God is perfect. It is the person's own wrong perception and hasty, impatient expectations. If the person experiences frustrations from humans, then this could also be the same problematic perception of this person or possibly the imperfection and faults of these humans.

99. The Fried Chicken, the Mother, and the Sufi

There was a famous Sufi who was eating a nice fried chicken. He had a student next to him, eating hard, non-tasty bread. The mother of the poor student entered the room to check on her child. As she saw this scene, she got very angry and said:

"Shame on you, teacher! You are eating a nice fried chicken and my poor son is eating hard bread. Is this fair? Is this what you teach?" The teacher smiled and said to the chicken, "Kumbiiznillah, ... Be alive with the permission of God." The chicken became alive and the mother was shocked and scared. The teacher said, "When your son is at this level, he can eat whatever he wants."[18]

In practice, the disciples sometimes can experience different conditions to discipline their eating, sleeping, and talking. The goal is to minimize them but it takes practice. Once one can gain the ability of controlling oneself, one can enjoy physical and spiritual joys in different modes in their full capacity and purpose.

---

18. This story is attributed to A. Jilani, a very famous eleventh century Sufi scholar and teacher.

100. Eating Meat and the Sufi

There was a Sufi who did not prefer to eat meat. One day, a Sufi friend of hers visited her and they started eating dinner together. There was a nice rotisserie chicken on the table. Her friend realized that she was not eating the chicken and she asked the reason. The Sufi smiled and said: "I don't know how and where this chicken spent its life . . . "

In practice, eating meat, chicken, or fish is permissible. But some Sufis pursue a vegetarian approach for self-discipline as a personal preference. Some may only prefer to eat organic, clean, unprocessed, and especially spiritually blessed food. Therefore, they may not eat food unless they themselves raise, buy, or sometimes cook it. Some may not eat because they believe that the negativity or lack of spirituality of the person who cooked the meal can have a bad effect on the meal. Some Sufis believe that reciting "BismiAllah, with the name of God" can remove all of these negative effects and they can move on to eat whatever they are offered. So, it is a matter of personal preference.

101. Cat and the Garage Door

There was a Sufi who had a cat. This cat wanted to leave the house to go to the garage when the door was open. The Sufi did not want the cat to go to the garage because it was not a natural environment compared to the backyard. The cat was insistent every day. One day, the Sufi said to her cat, "Fine, you can go." The cat went to the garage. After a minute, the cat came back to the door meowing and asking her to open the door. The Sufi was busy and delayed in opening the door and the cat continued meowing and crying. At the end, after a few minutes, the Sufi opened the door and said to the cat, "I hope you learned your lesson. This happens exactly between people and God."

Sometimes, a person may insist upon and want to do something that he or she may not realize is harmful. God may not give what the person is asking for due to its expected bad outcomes. But the person insists, even blames God, that God is not answering this person's prayer. Similarly, the cat in the above story insisted on something that the Sufi knew would be scary and bad for the cat. The cat insisted and the Sufi opened the door. After the cat's own experience, the cat went back to its home and knocked on the door with crying and meowing and the door was opened. When the person understands one's mistake, the door of repentance and going back and knocking at the door of mercy of God is always open. As long as the person is not in the state of arrogance and distractions, the person can re-establish beautiful connections with God.

102. The Sufi and Understanding His Wife

There was a Sufi. He was often upset that his wife was not spending much time with him as they grew older in their marriage. He was thinking about this. As he was reflecting on the marital problems of others, he realized that he had some similar problems. One night, he was disturbed by this and woke up in the middle of the night and prayed[19] in order to receive some guidance from God. At the end, he said, "Alhamdulillah, I got it. Men can become more sensitive as they grow older and expect more attention like a child. As men get older they don't feel that they have enough attention from their wives. Then, they can make a problem and even get divorced with different blames. Women can be more independent and still maintain the rationality compared to men. Therefore, I see a lot of men being taken care of by their wives in their old age. I think this is the root of my problem. Allah knows the best."

In practice, it is important to correctly detect one's own problems and disturbances through self-reflection and focus. In Sufism, there is a lot of advice recommending to solve problems at night while people are sleeping through prayers and invocation to God. In the above story, the Sufi got guidance to rationalize the source of his problem. Therefore, he can now discipline his own perception in his marital relationship.

---

19. Night prayer is called tahajjud.

103. "Staying Out of Trouble" and the Sufi

There was a man who used to come to the mosque. He was very friendly and always seemed very happy. Each time the Sufi saw this man, he used to say, "I am trying to stay out of trouble." The Sufi used to smile and think about what he meant. One year passed, two years . . . and more. Each time the Sufi saw this man, he would say, "I am trying to stay out of trouble." One day, the Sufi had a car accident. He smiled and understood why the man kept repeating this phrase. The Sufi said to himself, "Having a day without any problem is a blessing and requires gratitude to God."

Sometimes, a person may expect extraordinary things in life in order to be thankful to God on the journey. One can understand the value and happiness of the previous day when experiencing a difficulty or a problem in the present day. Therefore, a day without any evil or problem can elicit thankfulness and gratitude to God.

104. The Sufi, Child, and Disturbance

There was a Sufi in the mosque studying and praying. A child came with his father to the mosque. The boy was watching a cartoon on a smartphone and it was very loud. The Sufi was so disturbed. He was not able to focus and meditate. He was thinking about what he should do. He then pulled a small chocolate bar from his pocket and approached the boy and gave it to him and started praying next to him. The boy then muted the cartoon movie. The Sufi said, "Alhamdulillah . . . thanks and all gratitude is for God."

In practice, it is very important not to break anyone's heart when correcting or advising. Therefore, it is more important to think about how to say something compared to what to say. It is very strongly believed that the virtual space formed by manners remains, not the content of the talk or advice in human communication.

105. The Sufi and the Floating Wood Log on the Sea

There was a physicist Sufi walking on the seashore with his friend. While enjoying their walk, they saw a wood log on the sea, floating nicely on the sea's surface. The physicist Sufi asked his friend, "Why do you think this log does not sink?" His friend thought the Sufi expected an answer from physics because he was a physicist and continued explaining all the laws of physics . . . Then, the Sufi physicist said, "Actually, the wood log does not sink because it does not panic." His friend smiled . . .

In practice, there are always external and internal meanings to every minute detail of life. In the above story, although the wood log was very heavy, it did not sink and was nicely floating. The Sufi imagined a person's reasons, reactions, reasoning, feelings, and thoughts when they encounter something fearful and stressful and get trapped in it and die. One can consider a person who can die while swimming if there is panic or stress. Similarly, in spiritual endeavors, knowledge and practice help the person to not die in fear-provoking or evil-looking incidents. Actually, the person can enjoy this situation if the person knows how to submit and surrender instead of suffering and dying from it, similar to the case of the floating wood log in the story above. This spiritual level may take time, and practice, and one may need knowledge. It may not be easy to adopt it in the beginning of the journey.

106. The Sufi and the Cat in the Hood of the Car

One day a Sufi came to his home at night and parked his car in the garage. He did not see one of his cats at home. After a while his wife came and she was screaming, "Where is the cat? Did you run over the cat? I can hear her meowing and crying!" The Sufi was disturbed and immediately ran out and they found that the cat somehow went inside the hood from the wheel side and was stuck in there. Both the Sufi and his wife were panicking, felt very sad, and did not know what to do. They were calling the town for emergency animal rescue centers and friends. There was no help. Finally, they called the fire department and they came. After an hour, they were not able to get the cat out and suggested that the car should be torn down by a mechanic. They suggested that in the meantime, they should put some water and food next to the car in the garage, in case the cat comes out by herself to eat it. The Sufi and his wife were still very worried and panicking about the life of the cat. They continued calling multiple possible sources of help: AAA vehicle service, emergency mechanics, friends . . . They were on their way . . . While waiting for the help, the Sufi's wife opened the house door and screamed, "Mazza!" (the name of the cat). The cat was outside the door and she was OK. The wife started crying. The Sufi said, "Alhamdulillah, all thanks and gratitude is to God." In the meantime, he was also thinking . . . "Why my car? Why that cat . . ." He was trying to glean a meaning from this incident.

In practice, everything happens with a purpose, with a meaning, and a message for the person. In that sense, Sufis adopt a deterministic world approach. Therefore, some Sufis like the emerging theory of physics, the string theory. According to this theory, everything in the universe has a connection and effect on each other. For example, a butterfly's motion has an effect on the galaxies in the universe. Similarly, God sends different external messages to decode, guide, and connect with the Divine on the journey.

107. Final Stage of the Fireworks and the Sufi

There was a Sufi who was a giving a lecture. One of the students, who was in his seventies, asked a question. He revealed that he is having more spiritual experiences as he grows older in age and he asked the reason for this. The Sufi smiled and said, "In the fireworks show, there are more extensive displays as it approaches the end. Similarly, every journey has an end. As it gets close to the end, the signs may increase."

As all journeys have an end, the spiritual journey also has an end according to the practice. The ending of the spiritual journey is bound to the external ending of the physical journey of life. In other words, when the person dies, the first part of the journey ends. As the person is coming closer to the final stage of the spiritual journey, the signs may increase. Similar to the fireworks mentioned in the story above, during the last stage of the show, more intense and colorful fireworks may appear.[20]

The moments of experience, life-changing incidents, the avenues of enlightenment . . . All these signs may come in abundance as the person grows older. Depending on the person's attitude, the person can realize and decode these signs, or move on and perhaps still not understand.

---

20. The verse alludes to this notion (Sa nurIhImayatuna fi anfusihim and . . . hattayatabayannaannahulHaq).

108. The Sufi and the Oppression

There was a man and he had a daughter who was a Sufi. The father sometimes used to yell at his daughter and would not allow her to explain herself. One day, the father picked up his daughter from school and again started yelling at her and giving her some unsolicited advice. While they were driving, from out of nowhere, a car appeared next to their car and the father opened the window. The lady driver in the other car was angry and started cursing at the father and even said, "I will have my man find you and kill you." The father did not understand what was going on. He closed his window and kept moving. After a day, the Sufi daughter said to her dad, "Dad! I think yesterday, you didn't let me speak and you were yelling at me. Allah sent this lady from nowhere and she started cursing at you." The father regretfully said, "I think you are right. I am also thinking about that, too."

In practice, everything that happens to the person has a reason. Nothing is random. Nothing is chaos as long as the person knows the meanings. The person should follow the natural laws created by God as a means of respect to God. However, he or she should remember that in a limited human life everything is a sign to improve oneself on the journey and ultimately to better the relationship with Allah. Therefore, miracles are those incidents that break the natural laws to remind the person that everything is under the control of God. For a Sufi, if the person is attentive, mindful, conscientious, and sincere on the journey, then everything can continuously reveal itself with their miraculous real meanings.

109. Crying, Child, and the Sufi

A Sufi mother had a daughter and son. The daughter was older than the son. The daughter used to be mean and at time mentally abuse her younger brother. One day, the son wanted to take chips to school to share with his friends. The Sufi mother told her daughter to help her brother get the chips from the pantry. His sister did not let him and said, "He cannot get what he wants . . . " The younger brother started crying and tears were flowing down on his cheeks . . . The Sufi mother saw this and said to her daughter, "You shook the throne of God."

In practice, breaking someone's heart is similar to shaking the throne of God. In several sayings of the Prophet Muhammad, it is said that Allah is with the ones whose hearts are broken and who are oppressed. Therefore, the Prophet says, "Stay away from the prayer of the oppressed against you." In other words, if an oppressed person makes a prayer against another person, there is no hindrance for that prayer to be accepted.[21] In the above story, the mother alluded to those teachings for her daughter so that she could pay attention to her younger brother's needs.

---

21. Hanbal, Ahmad B. 2012. *Musnad Imam Ahmad Ibn Hanbal.* Dar-Us-Salam Publications. This is also one of the sayings of the Prophet.

110. The Sufi, Body, and Mindfulness

There was a Sufi who was trying to practice mindfulness with his body parts. Most of the time the taste faculty of the tongue in his mouth and his stomach were in conflict. Usually, his taste faculty in his mouth wanted to eat unhealthy, yet delicious food in abundant quantities. However, his stomach was telling him, "I don't want it. I will be the one who is going to suffer." The Sufi was using his mind and logic in decision-making when there was a conflict. Most of the time, he was deciding in favor of his stomach in his judgment, arrived at with his mind. One night, the Sufi was little bit depressed and upset, so he opened the fridge. The same dialogue started between his tongue and stomach. The Sufi's mind said, "I don't care about you, stomach. I will listen to the tongue this time." He started eating, and eating . . . Finally, he stopped. The Sufi suffered all night . . .

In practice, depending on the level of the person, it is important to have awareness about one's body parts. In other words, personalizing them, trying to understand each organ's needs and communicating with them through awareness is a level on the journey. This approach is also supported by the Quranic verse that the body parts would complain and witness against the person and talk on the Day of Accountability after death in front of God.[22]

Sufi, body, and mindfulness

---
22. In the chapter 41, verse 21.

111. Art of Living and the Sufi

One day the Sufi woke up to the sound of his wife screaming at the kids. She was trying to rush the kids to their extracurricular program. His wife didn't seem to be in a good mood. She finally left with the kids to drop them off, and then came back home around ten minutes later. The Sufi immediately woke up and said to himself, "Let me leave as soon as possible before I get hit by the storm!" (meaning his wife.)

He successfully left without bumping into his wife. On the way, while driving, he said to himself, "Alhamdulillah, thanks and all active gratitude is to God." A few minutes later, he received a long phone text from his wife. As soon as he saw the length of the phone text, he guessed the content of it, probably not something pleasant. Without looking at the message, the Sufi wrote, "Honey, I hope you are okay. I love you." A few hours later, he called his wife. Everything seemed normal and she was calm.

In practice, it is an art to not be pulled into arguments. It is very important to avoid any environments and instances that can be unpleasant. It is a level to recognize the other's disturbances and spiritual states before engaging with them. In the above story, the Sufi was spiritually skilled to consider the possible evil outcome of the incident.

The happy Sufi

SUGGESTED READINGS

Al-Ghazali, M. *Deliverance from Error*. Fons Vitae, 2000.
Al-Ghazali, M. *Ihya 'Ulum al-Din.'* Dar al-Fikr, 2004.
Al-Ghazzali, M. *On the Treatment of Anger, Hatred and Envy*. Kazi Publications, 2003.
Al-Ghazzali, M. *The Alchemy of Happiness*. Routledge, 2015.
Ali, A. Y. *The Meaning of the Glorious Quran*. Islamic Books, 1938.
Anjum, Z. Iqbal: *The Life of a Poet, Philosopher, and Politician*. Random House, 2015.
Arberry, A. *Interpretation of Koran*. Macmillan, 1955.
Arberry. *Muslim Saints and Mystics: Episodes from Tadhirat al awliya of Faird al-Din Attar, Omphaloskepsis*, 2000.
Asad, M. *The Message of the Quran: Translated and Explained*. Al-Andalus Gibraltar, 1980.
Avery, K. S. *A Psychology of Early Sufi Sama: Listening and Altered States*. Routledge, 2004.
Awang, R. "Anger Management: A Psychotherapy Sufistic Approach," vol. 9, no. 1, 2014, pp. 13–15.
Barks, C. *Rumi: Bridge to the Soul*. Harperone, 2007.
Barks, R. N. C. with J. Moyne, Rumi, Jelaluddin. "The guest house." *The Essential Rumi*. Harper, 1995, p. 109.
Bayrak, T. *The Name & the Named*. Canada, 2000.
Berguno, G. & Loutfy, N. "The Existential Thoughts of the Sufis. Existential Analysis." *Journal of the Society for Existential Analysis*, vol. 16, no. 1, 2005.
Bowen, J. *A New Anthropology of Islam*. Cambridge University Press, 2012.
Clarke, M. "Cough Sweets and Angels: The Ordinary Ethics of the Extraordinary in Sufi Practice in Lebanon." *Journal of the Royal Anthropological Institute*, vol. 20, no. 3, 2014, pp. 407–25.

Cutsinger, J. S. *Paths to the Heart*. World Wisdom, 2010.
Douglas-Klotz, N. *The Sufi Book of Life: 99 Pathways of the Heart for the Modern Dervish*. Penguin, 2005.
Ernst, C. W. *Teachings of Sufism*. Shambhala Publications, 1999.
Esposito, J. *The Oxford Dictionary of Islam*. Oxford University Press, 2014.
Friedlander, S. *The Whirling Dervishes: Being an Account of the Sufi Order Known as the Mevlevis and its Founder the Poet and Mystic Mevlana Jalalu'ddin Rumi*. SUNY Press, 1975.
Geoffroy, E. *Introduction to Sufism: The Inner Path of Islam*. World Wisdom, Inc., 2010.
Gibran, K. *The Prophet*. Oneworld Publications, 2012.
Hanson, Y. H. "The Creed of Imam Al-Tahawi." Zaytuna Institute, California, 2007.
Hanson, Y. H. *Purification of the Heart*. Alhambra Productions, 1998.
Helminski, K. *The Knowing Heart: A Sufi Path of Transformation*. Shambhala Publications, 2000.
Izutsu, T. *Sufism and Taoism: A Comparative Study of Key Philosophical Concepts*. University of California Press, 2016.
James, W. "The Will to Believe." *New World*, 1896.
Jawziyyah, Q. *The Prophetic Medical Science*. Idara Impex, 2013.
Karamustafa, T. A. *Sufism*. Edinburgh University Press, 2007.
Katz, J. G. "Dreams, Sufism, and Sainthood." *Brill*, vol. 71, 1996.
Khan, Z. M. *Gardens of the Righteous*. Routledge, 2012.
Kumek, Y. J. *Practical Mysticism: Sufi Journeys of Heart and Mind*. Kendall Hunt Publishing Company, 2018.
Lewis, B. *Music of a Distant Drum: Classical Arabic, Persian, Turkish, and Hebrew Poems*. Princeton University Press, 2001.
Malak, A. *Muslim Narratives and the Discourse of English*. SUNY Press, 2007.
Morris, J. W. "Introducing Ibn 'Arabi's Book of Spiritual Advice." *Journal of the Muhyiddīn Ibn 'Arabī Society*, no. 28, 2000, pp. 1–17.
Pickthall, M. W. E. *Holy Quran*. Kutub Khana Isha'at-ul-Islam, 1977.
Ramji, R. *The Global Migration of Sufi Islam to South Asia and Beyond*. Brill, 2007, pp. 473–84.
Renard J. *Knowledge of God in Classical Sufism: Foundations of Islamic Mystical Theology*. Paulist Press, 2004.

Rumi, J. *The Essential Rumi.* Harper, 1996.

Schimmel, A. *Deciphering the Signs of God: A Phenomenological Approach to Islam.* State University of New York Press, 1994.

Siddiqui, A. "Sahih Muslim." *Peace Vision,* 1972.

Trimingham, J. S. *The Sufi Orders in Islam.* Oxford University Press, 1998.

Upton, C. *Doorkeeper of the Heart: Versions of Rabi'a.* Threshold Books, 1988.

Usmani, T. *An Approach to the Qur'anic Sciences.* Adam Publishers, 2006.

GLOSSARY

A'bd worshipper, servant, or slave

Accountability liability, especially in Sufism and in Abrahamic traditions, everyone has a free will or agency in this world but accountability for their actions in the afterlife in front of God

Adab good manners, especially in the relationship with God in Sufism

Adjective attribute, a phrase describing a noun

Adonai name of God in Judaism

Affair relationship

Agency acting as an agent or a carrier with free will

Alhamdulillah a chanted divine phrase of appreciation of God or Allah

Alienating isolating, separating, disconnecting

Alienating Images of God understandings about God that disconnects person to establish a regular relationship with the Divine or to follow a religion

Allah proper name of God in Islam

Allude explain, refer

Anger uncontrolled and chaotic human spiritual state

Aphorism sayings, proverbs in a culture, society, or belief

Appreciate thank

Appreciative with capital A, God

Arabic language, especially the language of revelation of the Quran

Arrogance feelings and actions of superiority

Ascension rising, especially in Sufism, increase of spiritual states in relationship with God

Assert claim

Astagfirullah a divine phrase of asking forgiveness from God and cleaning the heart

Attribute adjective, a phrase describing a noun, especially in Sufism

Attributes of God divine phrases describing God

Authentic original, genuine, true

Balance modesty, especially in Sufism, following the middle way

Behavior temporary nature of a person

Bismillah a divine phrase of starting something with the blessing of God

Book of Chant the Quran

Boost increase

Bowing down bending one's body, especially the act of respect by bending one's body, for God

Candy hard delight, especially in Sufism, the pleasures or miracles given to the person on the path of God

Caution carefulness, alertness, especially in Sufism, in spiritual manners not to be trapped by ego or self

Certainty knowing without doubt, especially in Sufism, knowing and experiencing without doubt

Chanting repeating, especially in Sufism, repeating the phrases with focus and experience

Chaos disorder and confusion, especially in Sufism (spiritual) chaos being in negative states of anxiety, stress, and purposelessness

Charge positive states of spirituality that makes the person happy, peaceful, and calm, especially in Sufism, filling oneself with divine knowledge and experience

Compassion loving and caring

Glossary

Confirming Book   the Quran

Confirming Scripture   the Quran

Conscience   internal instinct of distinguishing right or wrong

Consciousness   awareness

Constant   not changing, permanent, especially in practice, known as Reflective Attributes of God, where humans have an image but God has its source

Construction   formation of an abstract entity

Contract   squeeze

Convergence   similarity

Cookie   soft delight, small sweet cake, especially in Sufism, the pleasures or miracles given to the person on the path of God

Cosmology   knowledge about the origin and development of the universe

Covenant   agreement

Death   end of physical faculties of a person, especially physical versus spiritual death; the soul does not die but the body dies in understanding of physical death in Islam

Dedication   sincere constant effort

Deity   representation of the transcendent

Detox   discharge

Devout   pious, practicing

Dhikr   as one of the names of the Quran, or any type of chant to remember God

Discharge   negative states of spirituality that makes the person sad, stressed, and anxious, especially in Sufism, emptying oneself from all the temporal and worldly positive and negative attachments

Divine   transcendent

Doctrine   teaching

Dominance   control

Dream visions when one is sleeping or awake

Ego self, identifier of a person, especially in Sufism, raw and uneducated identifier and controller of a person

Elohim name of God in Judaism

Embodiment, versus embody making it part of one's character

Endeavor engagement, activities

Epistemology theory of knowledge

Ethical moral

Ethnographic based on observation

Etiquette good manners and respect, especially in Sufism, respect in the relationship with God

Evil anything that causes stress, sadness, or anxiety

Evil eye the belief of unknown effects of the human eye across different cultures, traditions, and religions, especially in Sufism the evil eye effects due to extreme hatred, jealousy, or oppositely, evil eye effects due to extreme veneration and love of someone

Expand enlarge

Experience internalization of knowledge

Experience or experiential knowledge all types of learning except from a book or a teacher, internalizing and personalizing the formal learning

Figurative unclear, secondary and metaphorical

Free Will free choice of a person in decision-making

Generous with capital G, God

Genre type

Genuine sincere, original, authentic

Ghazali philosopher, theologian, Sufi mystic, lived in twelfth century

Glorification the mental, spiritual, and maybe verbal act of describing God in an admirable way

Groundless fake

Habitual habit of doing something constantly

HasbiyaAllah a chant with a meaning of "God is sufficient for me"

Healthy Cookies beneficial extraordinary incidents, such as miracles in Sufism

Heaven a place of all maximized pleasures of bodily and spiritual engagements while being with God

Hell a place of punishment

Heretic abnormal person, especially in Sufism, a desired state of being to experience and know the Divine

Humbleness behavior of modesty in viewing oneself, especially in Sufism, accepting the weakness in one's relationship with God and not being disrespectful and arrogant to God

Humility character or trait of humbleness

Illa Allah "except Allah" or "except God"

Images of God understandings and experiences about God

Imitation trying without real understanding

Infinite God, the Unlimited

Informant a person who participates in anthropological research

InshAllah God willing, hopefully

Intention planning ideas before the action

Internalize making it part of one's character, trait, or nature in Sufism

Intrinsic internal

Islam name of a religion that emphasizes believing in one God and Jesus, Moses, and Muhammad to be the human prophets of the Creator

Jihad struggle, especially spiritual struggle within oneself

Joseph Prophet of God in Islam, Christianity, and Judaism

Journey struggles of following guidelines of a mystical school

Khidr mystical being who is sent by God at any time to help people in their problems; also believed to be the teacher of Moses in a mystical journey as mentioned in the Quran

Kitab the Quran

Knowledge theoretical understanding of something through education

La ilaha illa Allah there is no God except Allah, a critical Divine phrase of chanting in Sufism implying a spiritual charge and discharge

Literal clear and primary

Lord God

Lucifer Satan, mentioned in divine scriptures such as the Bible and the Quran

Majnun crazy or, especially in Sufism, heretic

Mantra a repetitive phrase or sound, especially used in Hinduism and Buddhism

Meditation deep focus especially with reflection

Memorization learning by heart

Mercy compassion and forgiveness

Middle way living a balanced life in spiritual and worldly engagements

Mimic imitate

Mind logic, reason, and rationality

Miracle incidents against the law of physics and against all natural sciences

Mosque temple of Muslims

Muhammad the Prophet of Islam

Musaddiq the Quran

Mystic a person who adopts the teachings of mysticism

Mysticism the knowledge of the transcendent

Glossary

Nafs   self in its raw form

Neat   tidy and in order

Negation   denial, especially in Sufism, emptying from the mind and heart the imperfect ideas and feelings about God

Neglectful   not giving the proper attention that is due

Notion   concept, idea

Ocean   a very large sea, especially in Sufism, represents God the Unlimited or God's Unlimited and Incomprehensible Knowledge

Odd   not even, unique, no equivalence

Olam   hidden, waiting to be discovered through experiential knowledge

One   with capital denoting the one and only Creator

Oppression   unjust action of the strong over the weak

Permanent   constant, not changing, not ending

Permanent   non-ending

Phenomenon   occurrence

Pious   devout, practicing

Poisonous Cookies   harmful extraordinary incidents, such as miracles in Sufism

Pollution   making something dirty

Popular culture   the ethnographic data gathered over the period of years among different Sufi communities

Preposition   a word that does not have a meaning by itself but has a meaning in relation to another word, especially in Sufism, prepositions having conceptual and terminological meanings when one describes the relationships with the Divine

Pronunciation   correct sounds of letters in a language

Prostration, versus to prostrate   the act of respect by putting one's face on the ground, especially in Sufism, humbling oneself for God by putting the face, the noble part of the body, on the ground

Qibla the direction where Muslims and Sufis turn when they pray

Quran sacred text of Muslims

Rabbinic related to the Rabbis, the priests, and teachers of Judaism

Recitation, versus to recite reading, versus to read

Reliance dependence

Repetition repeating

Reverence respect

Reward prize, payment, especially in worldly and afterlife rewards in Islam

Ritual practices in a religion or mysticism that have spiritual and divine value for a person

Ruku bowing down

Rumi great Sufi mystic

Saint the person who believed to be close to God

Sakina peaceful and calm feelings

Salawat names of the chants to remember teachers and their covenants with their students, especially the main teacher, the Prophet Muhammad and others, such as Abraham, Moses, and Jesus

Samad the One who does not need anything, but everyone and everything needs God

Satan the Devil, Lucifer, mentioned in divine scriptures such as in the Bible and the Quran

Scent perfume, nice smell

Scholar expert, especially in Sufism, the experts who practice what they teach (alim)

Scripture sacred book or sacred text

Self ego, identifier of a person, especially in Sufism, raw and uneducated identifier and controller of a person

Service ethical action of doing good for others and society

Glossary

Spiritual Journey struggles of following guidelines of a mystical school

State level, especially in Sufism, spiritual level

Struggle efforts to achieve a goal

SubhanAllah glorification of God, a divine phrase of chanting of spirituality implying a spiritual charge and discharge

SubhanAllahu wa bihamdihi a divine phrase of glorification of God

SubhanAllahul Azeem a divine phrase of glorification of God in the prostration posture

SubhanRabbiyalAzim phrase of glorification for God in the bowing posture

Submission natural acceptance of the uncontrolled and unseen

Sufi follower of Sufism

Sufism mystical path of Islam

Superstitious fake

Surrender involuntary state of acceptance of the uncontrolled and the unseen

Tahajjud night prayer

Talismanic unknown and indescribable effects of divine words and sounds

Taqwa respect of God

Taste pleasure, especially spiritual pleasure such as peace, calmness, joy, and happiness in Sufism

Temple worship place

Temporal ending

Temporal transitory

Temptation false ideas

The Curer God

The Divine God

The Forgiver a name of God in Sufism

The Friend a name of God in Sufism

The Helper a name of God in Sufism

The Lover a name of God in Sufism

The Peace Giver God

The Real God

The Real Maker God

The Reminder the Quran

The Source God

The Sustainer a name of God in Sufism

The Wise with capital W, God

Throne a figurative or metaphorical representation of dominion of God

Trait permanent character or nature

Tranquility peace and calmness

Transcendent beyond human limits

Transitory temporal

Transliteration writing the sounds of words or phrases in one language with an alphabet of another language

Union being together, especially in this book, goal and joy of being always in the presence of God

Unseen anything five senses cannot testify in scientific methods

Weak not having a physical strength to perform an action, especially in Sufism, not having spiritual strength to perform any action

Worshipper a person who regularly follows and practices rituals, acts of prayers

ACKNOWLEDGMENTS

I would like to thank all my unnamed teachers, friends, and students for their input, ideas, suggestions, help, and support during and before the preparation of this book.

I would like to thank Professor David Banks, faculty of the Department of Anthropology, State University of New York (SUNY) at Buffalo, for meeting with me daily to go over the manuscript. I would like to also thank Ms. Toni Hajdaj for all her editing and suggestions and comments. I would like to thank Ms. Torrie Johnson, project coordinator, and Mr. Brandon Burke, editor at Kendall Hunt Publishing Company for their help and patience during this book project.

Lastly, I would like to thank all of my family members for their patience with me during the preparation of this book.

ABOUT THE AUTHOR

Dr. Yunus J. Kumek is currently the religious studies coordinator at State University of New York (SUNY) Buffalo State. He has been teaching undergraduate and graduate courses in religious studies at SUNY at Buffalo State, Niagara University, and Daemen College. Before becoming interested in religious studies, Dr. Kumek was doing his doctorate degree in physics at SUNY at Buffalo, and published academic papers in the areas of quantum physics and medical physics. Then, he decided to engage with the world of social sciences through cultural anthropology and spent a few years as a research associate in the anthropology department of the same university and published a book about different cultures and beliefs of international teachers in America. Recently, he completed a postdoctoral fellowship at Harvard Divinity School and published books on religious literacy through ethnography and practical mysticism: Sufi journeys of heart and mind. Dr. Kumek, who remains interested in physics—solves physics problems to relax—enjoys different languages—German, Spanish, Arabic, Hebrew, Urdu, and Turkish—especially in his research of scriptural analysis. Dr. Kumek takes great pleasure in classical poetry as well.

INDEX

A

Alhamdulillah, 44, 60
Angel, 10, 15
Anger, 91
Animals, 39, 40
Answers to Questions, 60
Ant, 50
Apathy, 93
Appreciation, 48
Arguments, 34, 111
Arrogance, 18, 19
Attachment, 89
Attributes, 66
Attributes of God, 95
Authenticity, 81
Awareness, 110

B

Backbiting, 34, 44
Bad smell, 14, 15
Bad Word, 43
Barriers, 76
Bismillah, 199
Bitter, 25, 36, 37
Blessing, 79
Body, 110
Breaking, 46

C

Calmness, 91
Cats, 39, 40
Cause, 13
Certainty, 76
Change, 56
Chants, 65
Charge, 96
Communication, 104
Context, 84
Contraction, 27
Cookies, 4
Criticism, 57

D

Day, 25, 36
Death, 12, 24, 32, 107
Deceiving, 59
Detachment, 20, 89
Dimensions, 76
Discharge, 20, 68, 89, 96
Disciple, 99
Discipline, 63
Distraction, 11
Divine Attributes, 66
Divine Names, 66
Divine Phrases, 65, 67
Diving, 47
Divorce, 38
Dreams, 49

E

Eating, 30, 43, 96
Ego, 3

Empty, 20
Escape, 33
Escort, 78, 83
Etiquettes, 84
Evil, 9, 42, 71, 76, 90, 111
Evil Eye, 97
Exception, 29
Expansion, 27
Expressions, 61
External, 36, 74
Externality, 64

F

Fault, 31
Fear, 105
Final Signs, 107
Food, 43, 79, 96
Free Will, 74

G

Garlic, 14, 15
Generosity, 13
Genuine Teacher, 78, 79, 80
Genuineness, 68
Good and Bad, 71
Gratitude, 103
Grief, 32

H

Happiness, 89, 103, 111
Heart, 27, 104, 109
Heedlessness, 73
Help, 93
Helper, 93
Hiding, 22, 26
Humbleness, 18, 19, 80

I

Ignorance, 100
Inheritance, 69
Inner, 74
Intellectuality, 58
Intention, 1, 37, 55, 57, 85

J

Jealousy, 22
Judgment, 64

K

Karma, 72

L

Language, 65, 84
Lesson, 100
Levels, 99
Loneliness, 33
Longing, 86
Loss, 32

M

Magic, 70
Man and Woman, 102
Marriage, 5, 23, 98, 102
MashAllah, 97
Meanings, 61, 106, 108
Meanness, 109
Meat, 199
Memorization, 67
Mindfulness, 110
Miracle, 54, 21
Missing, 86
Mistakes, 31

Index

N
Names of God, 16, 95
Natural, 94
Nature, 94, 95
Night, 25,
Night Prayers, 102
Not Caring, 73

O
Ocean, 47
Onion, 14
Oppression, 108, 109

P
Pain, 42, 89
Panic, 105
Patience, 40
Peace, 91
Perception, 87
Permanent, 86
Perspective, 50
Phrases, 65, 67
Physics, 95, 105
Poems, 17
Pregnancy, 42
Problems, 102
Protection, 70
Pure, 71, 94

R
Raw Self, 75
Recognition, 2
Reflection, 95
Reincarnation, 80
Representations, 74

Rotation of Days, 72
Rotation of Evil and Good, 72

S
Satan, 58
Saved, 82
Saving, 87
Scripture, 4
Self, 3
Service, 18, 19
Shame, 1
Shouting, 45
Signs, 66, 107, 108
Silence, 35, 62, 87
Simplicity, 96
Sincerity, 698
Smell, 44
Songs, 17
Spiritual Disease, 6
Spiritual Levels, 99
Spiritual Pain, 89
Spiritual States, 73
Spiritual Ugliness, 7
Stress, 105
Submission, 41
Surrender, 41
Sweet, 37, 36
Sweetness, 25

T
Talking, 31
Teacher, 78, 79, 80, 99
Temporality, 86
The Contractor, 27
The Expander, 27
Thinking, 44

Thoughts, 53, 54, 59
Thrifty, 87
Time, 87
Trouble, 103

U
Ugly, 76
Union, 90
Unknowns, 76
Unseen, 10, 76

V
Value, 8, 28, 83
Veil, 76

W
Wife, 52
Wisdom, 51

www.ingramcontent.com/pod-product-compliance
Lightning Source LLC
Chambersburg PA
CBHW051527230426
43668CB00012B/1773